effective
communication

John Adair is currently visiting professor in Leadership Studies at the University of Exeter and an international consultant to a wide variety of organizations in business, government, the voluntary sector, education and health. He has been named as one of the forty people worldwide who have contributed most to the development of management thought and practice.

Educated at St Paul's School, John Adair has enjoyed a varied and colourful career. He served in the Arab Legion, worked as a deckhand on an Arctic trawler and had a spell as an orderly in a hospital operating theatre. After Cambridge he became senior lecturer in Military History and Leadership Training Adviser at the Royal Military Academy, Sandhurst before becoming Director of Studies at St George's House in Windsor Castle and then Assistant Director of the Industrial Society. Later he became the world's first professor in Leadership Studies at the University of Surrey. He now writes extensively on leadership, management and history, as well as working as an international consultant.

John Adair is married with three children. He lives near Guildford in Surrey.

Other titles in John Adair's
Effective Leadership and Management series:

effective time management
effective decision making
effective teambuilding
effective leadership
effective motivation
effective innovation
effective strategic leadership

All are available from Pan Books,
priced £6.99.

John Adair

effective

communication

**THE MOST IMPORTANT
MANAGEMENT TOOL OF ALL**

PAN BOOKS

First published 1997 by Pan Books
an imprint of Pan Macmillan Ltd
Pan Macmillan, 20 New Wharf Road, London N1 9RR
Basingstoke and Oxford
Associated companies throughout the world
www.panmacmillan.com

ISBN 978-0-330-34786-0

9 8 7

A CIP catalogue record for this book is available from
the British Library.

Printed and bound in Great Britain by
Mackays of Chatham plc, Chatham, Kent

CONTENTS

3 EFFECTIVE SPEAKING

4 BETTER LISTENING

INTERLUDE: THE CHARGE OF THE LIGHT BRIGADE

5 THE SKILLS OF WRITING

6 THE ART OF READING

PART TWO: COMMUNICATION AT WORK

7 PRACTICAL PRESENTATION SKILLS

8 SUCCESSFUL INTERVIEWS

9 LEADING EFFECTIVE MEETINGS

10 ORGANIZATIONS: THE HIMALAYAS OF COMMUNICATION

INTRODUCTION

Communication skills are essential in leading, managing and working with others. The aim of this book is to help you to improve your competencies and capability in the art of practical communication.

An understanding of the NATURE OF COMMUNICATION is the foundation, and that is the subject of the first chapter. The five case studies that follow both illuminate some of the major communication problems and point the way forward to solutions.

The four skills, SPEAKING, LISTENING, WRITING AND READING, form the themes of Chapters 3, 4, 5 and 6. Of course we all have grounding and ability in these skills, and so it is more a matter of sharpening and honing them in the context of daily working life. If you aspire to lead or manage others you do have to be really competent in these skills, because communication is the brother or sister of leadership.

Three situations which pose problems of communication in which you will find yourself as a leader are discussed in Part Two. INTERVIEWS are essentially one-to-one meetings with a purpose. From the communicating angle, perhaps the most difficult aspect is giving and receiving praise and criticism. Managing communication in group MEETINGS is obviously an essential part of any manager's work. Lastly, ORGANIZATION – the general situation or context of managerial work – solves some communication problems but creates others.

It follows that to be an effective communicator, you need to develop an understanding of your PERSONAL skills, your ability to lead communication in GROUPS and your effectiveness in the downward, upward and sideways flows of information and ideas in ORGANIZ-ATIONS – including, of course, the interactions of the organization with its customers. Here, then, are the contents at a glance:

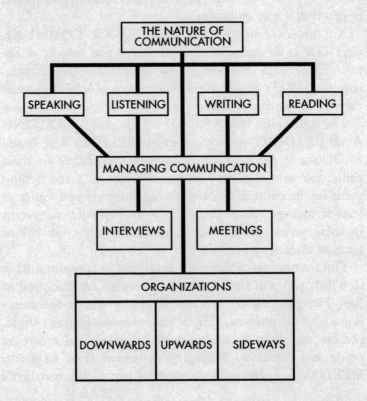

Remember that the purpose of the following pages is to stimulate your own thoughts and ideas on communication at work. They should lead you to identify some practical ways in which you can improve your skills both as a communicator and as a manager of communication.

HOW TO USE THIS BOOK

In order to get the most from this book it is best to read it once to get a general understanding. Then go back and work through the checklist questions and exercises. If you can persuade a friend or colleague to monitor your answers, so much the better.

Do not assume you have to start from the beginning and read through to the end. Even within a chapter you may prefer to complete the *checklists* in most chapters *before* reading the chapter rather than afterwards. Decide your strategy for using the book now, according to your depth of interest and preferred method of learning.

I suggest that you have a pencil and paper at hand when you study the book more closely. Write down any action points. Don't be afraid, of course, to write on the book – I won't mind! Underline or mark any passages which are important to you personally in terms of your own AWARE-NESS, UNDERSTANDING and SKILL.

This book will give you guidance not only on *when* to communicate and *why* it should be done, but also *how* it should be done. It is concerned with skills in a wide sense, namely the *methods* you must practise in order to achieve your desired aim of becoming a better communicator. But this book will not teach you much about techniques in the narrower sense which are often taught at the expense of the art of communication as a whole. Concentrate on the basics – and leave the tricks-of-the-trade to the charlatans!

In order not to hold you up unnecessarily on your first fast-track read, I have enclosed some material – relevant research and other contributions – in BOXES within the text. Again, be selective about them. You can skip them without any loss to the main themes of the book if you prefer.

The KEY POINTS at the end of each chapter are designed to give you an *aide-mémoire* of the whole contents. Just to keep you on your toes I have occasionally slipped in one or two extra points – ones you won't find in the preceding chapter.

I hope you enjoy reading the book as well as finding it useful and profitable. I have certainly enjoyed writing it.

John Adair

PART ONE

COMMUNICATION SKILLS

1

THE NATURE OF COMMUNICATION

'Our communication has just been criticized again,' shouted the irate Chief Executive at his startled executive directors. 'Look at this Customer Satisfaction report!' He flung down a thick report with POOR COMMUNICATION highlighted in yellow on the front summary. 'And our suppliers are none too happy,' muttered the Production Director to the Marketing Director. 'I want it improved by next Monday,' the Chief Executive roared, banging the table to emphasize his point, and walked out.

The senior executives left the meeting mystified. 'What does he mean by communication?' mused the Human Resource Director. 'We have got briefing groups, a new telephone system, a company newsletter, a hotline for dissatisfied customers.' 'How about a few more meetings?' suggested the Finance Director. 'I could manage breakfasts on the first Thursday of the month . . . We don't know what you guys are thinking about. We could perhaps update each other on developments in areas.' One of the managing directors of the six business areas looked aghast. 'No more meetings for me!' he exclaimed. 'Besides, the Finance Department never stop telling us what more information they want. If you only let us alone to get on with the job we would have time to communicate!'

When the Chief Executive arrived home at nine o'clock with his usual bulging briefcase, he noticed there were no lights on in the house. On the kitchen table he found a note from his wife. 'Dear Fred, you will find your supper as usual in the oven. Sorry, but I am leaving you. I have been trying to tell you for years about my feelings changing, but you just don't listen. You have totally ignored me and immersed yourself in your career. I can't put up with it for another day. You just don't seem to know the meaning of the word communication. Good luck, Fred.'

WHAT IS COMMUNICATION?

These days it is so easy to use the word *communication* almost like a cliché, without any reflection upon its meaning – a mistake made by the Chief Executive in the cautionary tale above. Most people, however, are aware that communicating is more than talking – or talking more often – but despite so many books, manuals and videos on the subject, it is a concept that is still far from clear.

Look at the appearance of the word first. It's one of those rather cumbersome, long abstract words that derive from the ancient Latin, like verification, clarification, domestication, and so on. Many people naturally avoid such terms, especially if they do not come from educated backgrounds where the use of long words tends to be encouraged. Shorter and simpler Anglo-Saxon words, like *talk* and *listen*, are preferred by those not subjected to an education which stretches their vocabularies.

But *communication* serves as well as a useful portmanteau

or umbrella term; it embraces both talking and listening, and a good deal more. It's a general concept that has earned its place in everyday speech and therefore it is worth trying to understand it in some depth.

The word itself comes from the Latin verb *communicare*: to impart, to participate, to share. That in turn probably derives from *communis*, the source of the English word *common*. A piece of common land, for example, is one which all can share. You can begin to see how general a word *communication* is by origin. Indeed, in the early days, *communication* used to include the giving or bestowing of material things. In the course of time it tended to become restricted to the imparting or transmitting of things intangible or abstract, which is how we use it now. (Except for the archaic use in the Church of England context, where people *communicate* or make their *communion* when they receive the Bread and Wine.)

Do not, however, make a false dichotomy between material and abstract in this context, for they are almost invariably interwoven. We are givers and receivers of material things by virtue of being social and reciprocal human beings. But this exchange of material things is the vehicle for exchanging more intangible or abstract ones, especially, to use that indefinable word, *meaning* (for what is the meaning of *meaning*?)

Sally Richards, a single parent, has taken leave from work to look after her daughter Anna who is recovering slowly from a severe viral infection. Her mother, who has recently broken a hip, has also arrived recently to recuperate. Coming home from shopping she finds at the back door a box of fresh vegetables and a dozen brown farm eggs, with a note from a local farmer over the hill with his best wishes.

Even to perceive something passed to you as a *gift* implies grasping something that isn't material: the meaning or intention 'behind' it, as we say. This process is seldom conscious; it is so much part of our nature that it is usually unconscious, unless it is problematic. You won't have any problems in placing a Christmas present, signalled with red wrapping paper and silver ribbon and – just to make sure – your name on it with a message of good will, in the *gift* category. Sally Richards had a little more difficulty. Not that she mistook the gift for a grocery delivery for which she was expected to pay – she knew it was a gift. But she liked the young unmarried farmer, whom she had met at the village pantomime a week earlier. She had been uncertain about whether or not he was interested in her – at least, until this gift arrived. 'But I mustn't read too much into it,' she told herself. Then the telephone rang. 'Just checking to see if those are the vegetables you like . . . Any chance of meeting you for a drink some time this week?'

You will notice how soon words come into the picture. A dozen brown eggs on their own could mean anything. First the note, then the telephone call. Although almost anything can become a symbol, by far the most important set of symbols when it comes to communication is language or words, including numbers.

SIZEABLE CHANGE

Asda, the British chain of supermarkets is to change the way it describes egg sizes after complaints from customers who did not know if a size 1 was a large or small egg. The supermarket chain plans to replace the 0 to 5 scale with small, medium, large and extra-large sizes.

Words are still material or tangible but in a very abstracted way. A gorilla would find this page with its incomprehensible squiggles almost totally uninteresting (not so the box of vegetables). When you hear language and words you hear sounds, which again are material or tangible as air passes over vocal cords and out of the mouth, but this physical dimension is insignificant in comparison with the symbolic role of these connected and modulated noises. If you don't know the language that is being spoken, you are left with an unintelligible gibberish of sound utterances. The Greeks called their neighbours Barbarians because their language had strange ba-ba sounds in it. The Dutch in South Africa called the Nama people Hottentots because of the repetitive click consonants in their language.

Communicating usually implies both intention and means. In a sharper focus we could say that communication is essentially the ability of one person to make contact with another and to make himself or herself understood. Or, if you prefer a slightly more formal version, *communication is the process by which meanings are exchanged between people through the use of a common set of symbols.*

Now, intention and a common set of symbols (usually language) are immensely important factors but they should not be allowed to fill the whole picture. Emotions or feelings, for example, are non-material. They are certainly communicated, sometimes intentionally but more often not. Nor is a common set of symbols involved. Emotions often do not need words. You should always bear in mind this much broader backcloth of communication, which encompasses such phenomena as the unintentional and direct transfer of states of mind or feelings.

A second or supplementary example to emotion is provided by poetry in particular and art in general. It is perhaps a characteristic of all art – especially poetry – that more is communicated than the artist originally intended, if his or her intentions were at all clear. For the listener, reader or writer may find in a poem or picture meanings that the originator did not have in mind, or at least consciously. Hence the feeling that artists sometimes share with prophets, that they are the means or vehicle for some genius or spirit inside and beyond themselves which uses them to speak to others. That is almost a definition of being a poet or artist, as opposed to a writer of verse or a craftsman.

These phenomena are possible because our minds shade from conscious into unconscious (or depth mind, as I prefer to call it). The unconscious is not merely a repository of memories and a source of dreams: it is capable of analysing, synthesizing and valuing. It can therefore solve our problems, make our decisions and generate new ideas. Communication is sometimes directed towards and received by these subliminal levels of mind. Poetry in particular speaks in the picture-language of images and metaphors to our depth minds.

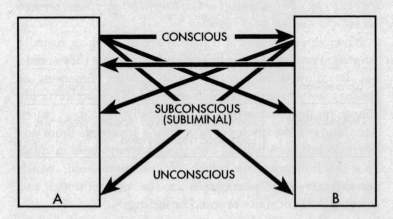

Figure 1.1   *Communication on different levels*

You can see from this model that once two or more people enter a kind of magnetic field between them, communication at a variety of levels, sometimes simultaneously, becomes possible. We are like radio sets in this respect, with a number of different channels and frequencies.

But let me return now to that central working definition of communication as the process by which meanings are conveyed or exchanged. You can see that there are four elements implicit within it. Of course, the whole process will always be more than the sum of these four parts, but each of them is an important factor in the overall story. In the table below, I identify them briefly and then a discussion of their characteristics follows.

KEY ELEMENT	NOTES
Social Contact	The persons who are communicating have to be in touch with each other
Common Medium	Both parties to communication must share a common language or means of communication
Transmission	The message has to be imparted clearly
Understanding	The message has to be received, properly understood and interpreted

Figure 1.2   *Key ingredients in communication*

I use the words *message* and *transmission* without enthusiasm, but I cannot think of better words. *Message* is roughly what you have in mind that you wish to communicate, while *transmission* – which suggests the mechanical metaphor of radio transmitters to me – simply covers the imparting of something so that what was once private mental property is now shared. Messages may be externally generated – information you have acquired – or internally generated, such as your own ideas or feelings or experience. There is no hard and fast division between these two categories. You may pass on some information – a mathematical principle, for example – in an undiluted form. In other instances you may make your own input, shaping or developing what you have received, before you pass it on to others.

SOCIAL CONTACT

Unless you are in contact with another person you cannot communicate. If there are undiscovered tribes in South America – or in outer space for that matter – neither you nor I can communicate with them. We are not connected. The most obvious form of connection is physical proximity – or being literally in touch or within touching range.

People who fit this category when we are at home are obviously our families, friends, colleagues and neighbours. But so is the stranger who stops you to ask the way, the telephone salesman who rings you in the evening or the engineer who comes to repair your washing machine. If you are overseas you will be in physical proximity to a lot of other people who are in effect total strangers by virtue of differences in language and customs.

Technology has transformed our situation by making it possible for us to establish social contact and to communicate over a distance of both time and space. The family of words formed from *tele* (the Greek for 'far off'), such as telegraph, telephone and television, signpost these technological innovations. Radio is another related development, as are film, video, tape and disc, telex, fax and computer links.

Historically, writing was the first of these breakthrough techniques, allowing letters and books. It is of course the technology I am using now. Although it is several thousand years old, it is still wonderful, however, that these words can be read and understood in distant parts of the world, possibly some years after they have been written.

If I may digress for a moment, one of the interesting and delightful things about being an author is to visit countries far afield and meet people who have read one's books. The odd thing is that some of these readers at least feel that they know you, that they have a relationship with you. I certainly have the same feeling about the writers whose books I like and admire.

The point that suggests itself to me here is that *communication tends to create relationship*. The more you communicate with someone the more likely it is that a positive relationship will develop. The converse is true. The stronger, better or deeper a relationship is, the more probable it becomes that communication within it will be good. As the proverb says, 'The wings carry the bird, but the bird carries the wings.'

A COMMON MEDIUM

A medium is a means of effecting or conveying something, a channel of communication. For us humans, the most obvious medium, as we have already agreed, is a language, such as English, French, Spanish or German. Language is integral to being a person. 'Nothing is more mysterious than the power of speech,' wrote Edward Thomas. 'It is the supreme proof, above beauty, physical strength and intelligence, that a man or woman lives.'

We have the genetic capacity to learn language, though of course the languages we learn are all different; they are reflective of the culture and age in which we are born and reared. (Genetics also relate to specific languages. My progress in Arabic is limited because I cannot roll my Rs nor manage a glottal stop. I doubt if I could master the tone differences in Chinese or the clicking consonants in the Bushman language.) Whether or not all languages evolved from one proto-language with a simple vocabulary of root words is a hypothesis that is yet to be proved, but certainly many languages are related in family groups and descend from common ancestors. Hence a Dutchman, for example, can more or less understand a Fleming.

THE ROOTS OF COMMUNICATION

We can perhaps learn more about the distinctive role of language in human communication if we glance first at the world of mammals, birds and fish; a world limited to non-verbal or non-linguistic communication. Wherever we look in the animal kingdom we find that communication without language is less liable to error than in humans but it is much more limited. Humans, with an infinitely richer potential, are capable of attaining a communion with their fellows and their universe which is beyond the reach of even the most developed animals. Yet human communications are much more likely to go awry than those of our evolutionary cousins and our more distant relatives in the family of the living.

In her study of chimpanzees, entitled *In the Shadow of Man*, the zoologist Jane van Lawick-Goodall emphasized that speech sets humans far ahead of their nearest primate cousins, but that we retain many of the primitive methods of communication observable in the chimp.

In fact, if we survey the whole range of the postural and gestural communication signals of chimpanzees and humans, we find striking similarities in many instances. It would appear then, that either man and chimp have evolved gestures and postures along a most remarkable parallel, or that we share with the chimpanzees an ancestor in the dim and very distant past; an ancestor, moreover, who communicated with his kind by means of kissing and embracing, touching and patting and holding hands.

One of our major differences between man and his closest living relative is, of course, that the chimpanzee has not developed the power of speech. Even the most intensive efforts to teach young chimps to talk have met with virtually no success. Verbal language does indeed represent a truly gigantic stride forward in man's evolution.

All the same, when humans come to an exchange of emotional feelings, most people fall back on the old chimpanzee-type of gestural communication – the cheering pat, the embrace of exuberance, the clasp of hands. And when, on these occasions, we use words too, we often use them in rather the same way as a chimpanzee utters his calls – on an emotional level.

It is only through a real understanding of the ways in which chimpanzees and men show similarities in behaviour that we can reflect, with meaning, on the ways in which men and chimpanzees 'differ'. And only then can we really begin to appreciate, in a biological and spiritual manner, the full extent of man's uniqueness.

A chimpanzee or an otter, however, is less likely to misinterpret one of its kind touching or clasping it in the presence of some anxiety-producing threat than, say, a pretty girl whose hand is suddenly held by her neighbour in a descending airliner. The repertoire of signs, gestures and postures is limited, and all the animals seem to know the code. Human nature greatly confuses the issue. Not only is human speech an infinitely varied weaving and interweaving of forty different sounds, but the resulting words are capable of many different interpretations. Hence a person can convey or communicate much more widely and more deeply than a chimp can with its fellows, but at the risk of being more misunderstood and more isolated than any in the animal kingdom.

Such studies as the one reported above suggest that there is a legacy from our evolutionary past. Despite our development of language we retain *non-verbal communication* as an important auxiliary system.

NON-VERBAL COMMUNICATION

The basic system for communication is the human body; not only the organs of speech and hearing, but eyes and facial muscles, hands and arms, brain and in many respects the entire body. Caressing, embracing and holding hands are as much ways of communicating as human speech. Body language, as it is now familiarly called, is something we both use and observe throughout our waking hours. Everyone, for example, can interpret a smile or a threatening gesture. And the voice conveys more through its tone or volume than simply the words spoken.

We can distinguish at least nine ingredients in this 'undercover language' of non-verbal communication. They are:

- facial expression
- eye contact
- tone of voice
- physical touch
- appearance (clothes, hair)

- body/posture
- proximity
- physical gestures, hand and foot movements
- head position

Take eye contact, for example. Video film of conversations shows that the talker tends to look away while actually speaking, but to glance up at the end of sentences for some reaction from the listener, which usually takes the form of a nod or murmur of assent. He or she gives the listener a longer gaze when the talk has finished.

For the most part this undercover language is a natural or unconscious expression of our feelings, synchronized with what we are saying or doing consciously.

It follows that one can only change non-verbal behaviour by changing the inner nature which it is expressing. Courses or conferences which aim to teach you what Shakespeare called 'the craft of smiles' are to be regarded with suspicion, although help can be given to those whose synchronization has become dysfunctional.

Courses for normal people in such matters as eye contact or gesture could only induce self-consciousness, which works against natural communication. What is important, however, is the *awareness* that other people are receiving all our non-verbal behaviour, and perhaps finding it expressive of certain unseen inner states or attitudes which may or may not be there. One can legitimately strive to avoid sending out the wrong signs or signals through the variety of non-verbal channels. Fortunately, we now have language, which can in part rectify our mistakes. But it is the original integrated combination of words and signs which makes up the rich texture of human communication. We must now turn to our unique capacity for communicating through language – the prime means of human intercourse.

THE ROLE OF THE ENGLISH LANGUAGE

One way of solving the problem of communication among different language speakers is to resort to sign language. Symbols may convey meaning more readily than words, and mean the same to virtually every nationality.

But this expanding number of international signs is self-evidently limited as a means of communication. The world stands in need of a common language.

To meet this need English has become increasingly significant in the league tables of language. It is not the language spoken by the most people in the world – Chinese has that distinction – but it is top of the list as a second language. Over a billion people can now speak English as their first or second language.

The value of such a common language has long been perceived. In the Persian empire, Aramaic performed that function. Greek played that role in the Graeco-Roman world of antiquity, and Latin took over into the Middle Ages, not least because it remained the common language of the Catholic Church. The 'Frankish tongue' – a mixture of Italian with French, Greek, Arabic, Turkish and Spanish, once used in the eastern part of the Mediterranean in the seventeenth century, gave us our phrase *lingua franca*, which now means any language serving as a medium between different nations with their own separate languages.

At first sight it may seem odd that English, the language of a relatively small group of islands off the European shore, should be rapidly becoming the *lingua franca* of our day. The fact of the British empire, which planted English in America, India, Africa and Australasia, had much to do with it. The adoption of English as the language for international purposes such as air traffic control is another factor. English is the language of the United Nations, of world banking, of diplomacy, of academic research, space travel, scientific discovery and global computing. Like the original *lingua franca*, of course, it is a mixture of Anglo-Saxon or Germanic, Norse, Greek, Latin, French and Arabic, together with other captive words from most main languages under the sun, which gives it an extraordinary richness.

Apart from its variety and flexibility, English has other inherent qualities. It has few inflections, endings or cases. Its grammar is based on simple word order. It has no clicks, tones or implosives. Its alphabet is phonetic and has 26 letters (against 74 in Khmer and 85 in Cherokee). A student of Chinese or Japanese must learn 2000 characters. English script can be scrawled and shorthanded.

TRANSMISSION

Granted social contact, whether immediate or at a distance, and a language understood by both parties, the communicator has to impart the message in an effective way. That requires, first, overcoming any physical obstacles and, second, expressing yourself clearly.

The first of these requirements is relatively easy for us today. We have all heard the injunction to 'Speak up!' You have to be heard in order to be understood. To speak clearly and distinctly increases the chances of being understood. If you cannot be heard, you cannot be understood. In earlier times, before the invention of the microphone, speaking to large audiences required a special training, such as only actors receive today. In fact the first British prime minister to use a microphone was David Lloyd George after the First World War. As technology improves, the reliability and quality of tele-instruments improve all the time. One day they may even make portable telephones work properly . . .

The second requirement is more complex, owing to the nature of language. Many words are not susceptible to a single definition, and so they are not good conduits of unambiguous meaning. It is necessary for communicators to be aware of these limitations in any language and to select words carefully in order to convey their exact meaning, where necessary explaining in what senses they are using a particular word. If you are offering *love* to a member of the opposite sex, for example, it is worth indicating what you mean by that concept in relation to this particular person! Although in the universe somewhere there may be a 'gold standard' for *love* there are so many perceptions and variants of the concept that even in the same culture you cannot assume the meaning given to it by the other person will correspond with your own.

Another way of making the same point is to say that all languages work by overtones – the associations or nuances which words acquire in their long histories. A good dictionary will tell you about this hidden luggage, suggesting the particular overtones that cling to words or concepts. Dr Samuel Johnson pointed out long ago when he compiled his dictionary that there were no synonyms in the English language. That should encourage us to search for what the French call *le mot juste*, the right word, even if we are not always successful in finding it.

Apart from the dictionary you will need to know about the 'receiver'. As most of our daily communication is with those who share the same native language and culture, we can usually be tolerably certain that our intentions and meanings in speech will be broadly understood. And, of course, relationship, with its deepening mutual knowledge, makes that a lot more likely. But it becomes much more problematic when you are speaking beyond the confines of family and associates, not to known individuals but to less known groups. For example, I know that for many readers of this book, either English will be a second language or else they will read it in their own language. How much meaning will be lost in translation? That depends on the skill of the translator, that trader in languages, but we all know that something will be lost. When I read the Koran in English, for example, the poetry of the original Arabic is largely lost.

Commercially the nuances of words can be an extremely important factor, as the following true story shows:

Edgar Giftware Enterprises decided to expand their marketing activities to France and Germany but conducted no market

research. 'Why should we?' the managing director explained.
'We have the most successful range of giftware in the United
Kingdom and we have been very successful in the United States
as well.'

Yet the English Heritage Giftware range, with its television
marketing slogan *A gift from England – a gift of a lifetime*,
produced only a disappointing response in Germany. 'Did no
one tell you?' asked a German television producer. 'The word
gift in German means a poison.'

For language is both the produce and guardian of a culture.
You need to understand the culture in order to understand
the language and vice versa. Dead languages, as we call
them, remain the archaeology of a civilization. I am
intrigued that there may once have been 2000 distinct
languages in South America, relics of the primeval grunts
that mankind brought across the Aleutian bridge from
Siberia in 10,000 BC. Few of them were recorded and only
some 600 still survive, most of them still unstudied. Like
all languages, their words contain countless images and
messages caught like flies in amber. Full of wisdom, legend
and beauty, these great human artifacts can still communicate with us or at least allow us to share vicariously in a
vanished culture.

UNDERSTANDING

Most people seem to regard spoken communication as
getting a message across to another person: 'You tell him
or her what you want them to know.' This concept implies
a one-way traffic from one person to another, with all
the emphasis being on transferring a message from one

mind to another. But communication is essentially a two-way process; it is shared or common activity. If you close your eyes in order to stop reading you will effectively end the communication between us. Quite apart from this basic willingness to receive, you have to be active as a listener or reader in order to grasp what is being said. Meaning isn't something conveyed like electricity from one mind to another; it is a magnetism created when two minds meet.

COMMUNICATION IS DIALOGUE

The monological argument against the dialogical process is that the ignorant and untutored have nothing to contribute, so that the addition of zero and zero equals zero.

This kind of comment, which is made by surprisingly intelligent and otherwise perceptive people, and too often by educators, demonstrates how little they know about the process of learning. Nor does it follow that the dialogical principle forbids the use of the monological method. There is a place for the lecture and for direct presentation of content, but to be most useful they should be in a dialogical context. Furthermore, it is quite possible for a person giving a lecture to give it in such a way that he draws his hearers into active response to his thought, and although they remain verbally silent, the effect is that of dialogue.

As a matter of fact, one should not confuse the different methods of teaching with the dialogical concept of communication. Both the lecturer and the discussion leader can be either monological or dialogical, even though they are using different methods. The person who believes that communication, and therefore education, is dialogical in nature, will use every tool in the accomplishment of his purpose. When the question needs to be raised, he may use the discussion method or perhaps some visual aid. When an answer is indicated, he may give a lecture or use some transmissive resource. But his orientation to his task is based on his belief that his accomplishments as a leader are dependent partly upon what his pupil brings to learning, and that for education to take place their relationship must be mutual.

Dr Reuel L. Howe, *Herein is Love*, Chicago, The Judson Press, 1961

The real fallacy of seeing communication as one-way traffic is that it ignores your and my contribution to the communication process. Monologue sees a passive audience; dialogue knows that the other person holds some of the cards that will give to or withhold meaning from both of us. Thus one of the outward signs of a person who is truly convinced that communication is dialogue is that he will be as much interested in knowing about the person with whom he wishes to communicate as he is in knowing about the subject in question.

Consequently an awareness of the other person or persons as active contributors to the 'commoning', and not as passive receivers, is an unseen *dimension* which can influence any form of communication.

THE ROLE OF FEEDBACK

The importance now attached to feedback belongs to this essentially dialogical concept of communication. Feedback is a metaphor from the electronic world. It means literally the return to the input of a part of the output of a machine, system or process. If you speak too close to a microphone you will often experience feedback. In a wider sense it means the partial reversion of the effects of a process to its source.

Where communication is intentional, and in order to achieve some effect, as it so often is, you may notice that sometimes no response is expected. A lot of everyday instructions fall into this category. For example, a sign in the street saying KEEP LEFT is looking for an effect but not a direct acknowledgement or response.

In higher or more complete forms of communication a response is usually either expected or elicited. It may or may not be followed by an effect, depending on the nature of the communication. If you ask someone what they think of your proposal you will certainly get a response, possibly in the shape of a lengthy discussion. But whether or not your proposal produces an effect is another matter.

> What do you think? A man had two sons; and he went to the first and said, 'Son, go and work in the vineyard today.' And he answered, 'I will not'; but afterwards he repented and went.
>
> And he went to the second and said the same; and he answered, 'I go, sir,' but did not go. Which of the two did the will of the father?

This parable of Jesus illustrates clearly the difference between *response* and *effect*. The initial positive and negative responses – or feedback – of the sons was no guide to the effectiveness of the communication. One moral of the story for leaders is *always judge your communication by its effect and not by response*. That almost involuntary reaction or feedback, of course, is still extremely important – not least because it is an early indicator of whether the intended effect is likely to be forthcoming.

KEY POINTS

- The concept of communication embraces a wide range of meanings circling around the idea of *sharing*. That sharing or exchange is now more commonly of abstract things, notably meaning.

- For communication to happen there are some necessary elements or conditions: social contact, a common medium, transmission and understanding.

- Some contact or connection is required. It may be physically close or (through technology) at a distance. If you are out of touch with people you can't communicate with them. But you may be out of touch because you don't communicate! Communication creates relationships; relationship produces communication.

- Although we have evolved language as our principal medium for communicating with each other, we retain non-verbal communication; just as a sailing yacht might have an auxiliary motor. It is especially important as an expression of relationship. In Japan as in African tribal society, for example, how near or far you sit from the door indicates your seniority.

- Both a distinct and clear transmission of some kind is required, and also an equal reception of it. Both 'sender' and 'receiver' contribute to the process by which meanings are exchanged between them by a common system of symbols.

Communication is the art of being understood.
Peter Ustinov

2

SOME COMMON
COMMUNICATION PROBLEMS

There is a tendency these days to ascribe failures in professional or personal life to 'problems of communication'. Sometimes that is an accurate diagnosis. Elsewhere, however, 'problems of communication' is no more than a cloak of rationalization for other causes. They are usually, anyway, someone else's fault. It takes honesty — occasionally a great deal of it — to admit even in principle that these communication problems are generated by the familiar person you see in the mirror every day.

Think of this chapter as a set of mirrors. You may catch a glimpse of yourself in one or two of them. For its aim is to help you to identify and think about your own major communication problems. Where does the shoe pinch for you?

If you do recognize yourself in some of these stories you will have taken a forward step in self-awareness and self-understanding. The rest of this book will then help you to convert that new energy into practical ways for transforming yourself into an effective communicator in all situations, not least in your work as a leader or manager. For the overall purpose of this book, as a reminder, is for you to improve your skills as a communicator as a result of reading, reflecting and reaching out from it to your own situation.

Therefore may I remind you that it's a good idea to have a pencil and paper at hand to jot down any thoughts that come to you as you read the case studies. First thoughts are sometimes best thoughts. These notes should form the basis for your own self-help improvement plan.

THE CASE OF THE INVISIBLE MAN

William Bolton invited me to sit next to him at a dinner on the last evening of the course. He was the vice-chancellor of the university, a medical scientist by background, and I had been running a leadership programme for heads of departments and university administrators of the region at his university.

'No, I don't let people come and see me without an appointment,' he was telling me, 'nor do I visit departments. I believe that keeping a good distance between me and the staff creates an aura of respect. Familiarity breeds contempt.'

'But what about communication?' I asked. 'Doesn't your policy of staying remote make that rather difficult?'

'Not really,' he replied. 'My secretary keeps me in touch with what is going on. Moreover, I believe that information is power. If you give information to others, you lose your power. I am the only one who knows the whole picture and I like it that way. Do you recollect how the British succeeded in ruling India for so long? By following the principle of *divide and rule*, and I do precisely the same here!' he added with a laugh.

Next morning one of the host university's heads of department commented to me over breakfast that it had been an unusual experience to see the vice-chancellor, let alone talk to him. 'I've only discussed things once with him in my two years here,' he added. 'We call him the Invisible Man. I expect he spends all his time on national research bodies and committees. No, he certainly does not communicate with us, except for a letter to all heads once a term if he's not too busy.'

William Bolton is offending against the first and most obvious principle of communication, namely, that in order to communicate you have to be in social contact with the other person or people. It would be no good sending him on a course in communication skills or techniques, or lending him this book. His problem is much more fundamental. He doesn't WANT to communicate.

You may think I have chosen an extreme case, but I did not invent the story of William Bolton. It does take us to the heart of the matter. At the core of becoming an effective communicator is the burning desire to be one. If you are not in love with good communication, read no further.

Can nothing be done to help William Bolton? For him it was too late – he retired soon after. But for you it is not too late. If you see yourself in this portrait and want to change yourself, you have to go back and challenge your own unconscious ambitions about the very nature of leadership and management. Bolton was in the role of a strategic leader but he was not a leader.

One of the most interesting findings of the research on leadership has to do with the ability of the leader to speak and write fluently. Language facility is a key factor in leadership. As Disraeli said, 'With words we govern men.'

Abraham Lincoln became famous for his simple and effective speech. He had a natural gift for the written and spoken word even though he was relatively uneducated. Of Abraham Lincoln, the *Cambridge History of American*

Literature says, 'Not his politics, not his course of action, had won for Lincoln his commanding position in his party in 1860, but his way of saying things. In every revolution there is a moment when the man who can phrase it can lead it.'

The idea that staying remote from your people creates an aura of authority, a charisma which invokes awe, fear and respect, occurred first in the ancient Persian empire. It led to the elaborate rituals of monarchy, designed by a process of distancing to invest ordinary mortals with the numinous quality of the gods. Central to the formula was a strict rationing of royal appearances. William Bolton was unconsciously modelling himself on the Persian emperors and their successors.

This model, however, conflicted with the Greek idea of charisma. The Greeks saw leadership as a gift given by the gods and developed by education. The Greeks expected their leaders to be both better than them – the perception of betterness – but also one of them: *primus inter pares* or first among equals. Alexander the Great exemplified this ideal of a Greek king or leader who worked, fought, slept, feasted, marched and suffered among his men. To the Greeks – as naturally free and equal people – the Persian idea of a great social distance between leader and people, allowing the former to be revered as a god, was the antithesis of all their values.

But what about William Bolton's point that familiarity breeds contempt? True, so it does. Yet you can be among people without being familiar in the pejorative sense. Being in the leadership role itself, for example, does create a certain psychological distance, whatever the degree of physical proximity. Moreover, leadership involves risks. Surely it is better to risk familiarity than be condemned to remoteness with all its dangers of poor communication?

> In the Western Desert during the Second World War, Winston Churchill once took General Auchinleck for a walk and asked him why he didn't get away from headquarters and spend more time with the troops. 'Prime Minister, I don't have time,' replied the general, 'and anyway I believe that familiarity breeds contempt.' Churchill thought for a moment, chuckled and replied, 'In my experience, General, without familiarity you cannot breed anything!' Not long afterwards Auchinleck was replaced by Montgomery, a general with a passion for good communication with the soldiers.

Notice also William Bolton's assumption or belief that information is power. His strategy for maintaining his own power was not to share information. In other words, he had a reason for not wanting to communicate. Now it's just possible that you may share – however unconsciously – Bolton's reasoning and that may be why you are more a reluctant than an effective communicator. But remember that you will never have so much power as when you give it away. And the best way to empower others is to impart information together with the authority (subject to your overall responsibility) to decide and to act upon it.

As a leader you need to get out of your office as often as you can. Delegate as much of the paperwork as possible. Nelson had cleared his table of all correspondence and administration before breakfast, so he could be free to lead, to decide and to communicate throughout the day. Get out where the action is. Meet people and listen to what they have to say. Impart the whole picture to them: it will give them the vital context and the compelling reason why for all their efforts and strivings. Encourage them, for encouragement is the oxygen of the human spirit.

THE CASE OF THE UNHAPPY CUSTOMER

When Sally Brompton won a prize of £20,000 in the National Lottery, it seemed as if a family dream was about to come true. Both her husband Mike and herself, together with their two children Mark and Stephen, were keen bird watchers, and Mike had often joked that if he ever won the football pools he would treat them all to a bird-watching holiday in Zimbabwe during the migration season, and so it was with some considerable excitement that she picked up the telephone and dialled . . .

'Enterprise Africa Holidays here, what can we do for you? Two weeks in Zimbabwe – major game reserves – bird watching on Lake Kariba and the Zambesi – must be home by the end of August when your husband starts a new job. Yes, Mrs Brompton, we've got all that. We will send you an itinerary and an all-in price. It will be a pleasure to arrange it all for you. You are wise to plan well ahead this year. Thank you for calling.'

Days passed. After six weeks, Sally called Enterprise Africa Holidays again. They seemed a bit vague. Someone in the office remembered the call but Kevin had dealt with it and he had left. Maureen would look into it and call back. All would be taken care of. Silence.

After another three weeks the itinerary finally arrived, with the order of the game reserves changed and the return home delayed by two days, which would mean the extra expense of hotels in Harare.

'Unfortunately, Mrs Brompton, we had to change the itinerary because some of the internal flights in Zimbabwe are no longer available. You see, the All-African Games are being held in

Harare this year and so there is unusual pressure on both flights and hotels. And had you booked a bit earlier we could have got you some attractive discounts on the international flights but now you have left it so late you will have to pay the full economy fare. Sorry, too, about those extra two days in Harare, you see both British Airways and Air Zimbabwe took their last bookings on the flights you originally wanted about ten days ago . . .'

Sally put the telephone down. 'I just cannot believe it,' she said and burst into tears.

Customer Care has become a bit of a cliché these days. Everyone aspires to it; a few actually do it; and still fewer do it excellently, consistently and from the heart. For, as the Bedouin saying goes: 'What comes from the heart is greater than what comes from the hand only.' Or, we may add, the mouth. For so often Customer Services is lip-service.

Good communication is the core of customer care, just as it is the core of harmonious and progressive human relations within your organization. Customers and – we must add – suppliers are both vital to your business success. To turn satisfied into delighted customers should be your aim, whether you employ a host of people or only yourself. For if you are self-employed it is helpful to see yourself as a business, and therefore you are under that same inexorable law of finding and retaining customers – literally people who come back a second and more times.

This is common sense, you may say. But common sense, as they say, is not always common practice. It wasn't for Enterprise Africa Holidays Ltd. That firm showed no interest in communicating with Sally Brompton. Perhaps they didn't want her custom. If so, they should have said it at the outset. But they led her to believe they would take care of her. As a result they created an extremely dissatisfied and unhappy customer. It's always good practice to keep customers and suppliers informed of what is going on. If there are delays or problems, explain what they are and what you are doing to solve them. People appreciate regular and unsolicited progress reviews.

Every business now has to seek competitive advantage. In all industries, especially service industries, those who can communicate to good effect with their customers or clients in the way I have outlined above will always enjoy competitive advantage. Your competitors will divide into two groups:

* those who take their customers for granted and place no value on sustaining good communication with them
* those who can read the writing on the wall and are striving to catch up with your standard of customer care

You need not fear the former, at least not until they are taken over and are subject to demanding new business leaders. As for the latter, by the time they have reached where you are today, you should be much further up the road. What plans has your organization for improving communication in the next twelve months?

CHECKLIST: DO YOU COMMUNICATE EFFECTIVELY WITH YOUR CUSTOMERS?

	Yes	No
Have you had any complaints from customers in the last three months about the quality of the products or services you supply?	❏	❏

CHECKLIST: DO YOU COMMUNICATE EFFECTIVELY WITH YOUR CUSTOMERS? (Cont)

	Yes	No

If a major customer expresses dissatisfaction do you
– send them a letter or fax? ☐
– speak to them on the telephone? ☐
– arrange a face-to-face meeting? ☐

Do you communicate any changes in products,
levels of service and price well in advance of
actually making them? ☐ ☐

Can you list five ways in which you try to stay close
to your customers and their needs?
1
2
3
4
5

Have customer suggestions – listened to and acted
upon – resulted in any product/service innovations
within the last twelve months? Specify what they are. ☐ ☐

Have you a plan to improve customer care? ☐ ☐

I almost forgot to mention it, but there is a reward for good customer communication. If you meet their needs your customers will communicate about you favourably to other would-be customers. Word-of-mouth recommendation is the most powerful marketing tool in the world. And it costs you nothing.

THE CASE OF THE NERVOUS SPEAKER

A black cloud on the horizon. After five hectic but successful years as a bond dealer in the bank, Jennifer Huxley was applying for the post as head of the new marketing department in the corporate finance division. It was a big step but she felt well prepared for it. She had been a team leader for two years. Her university degree had been in economics and business studies, with an emphasis on marketing, and despite a busy social life she had done part-time study to obtain a specialist qualification in marketing financial institutions. She had already worked closely with the corporate finance division and one of her friends there had told her over a drink that she was seen as the leading internal candidate. But there was one snag . . .

The bank's specification for the job mentioned 'a strong confident personality who is an excellent communicator and presenter'. To test presentation skills the Corporate Finance Director and his senior colleagues had asked the five short-listed candidates – including Jennifer – to present a marketing strategy for the next three years to them. It wasn't the content that bothered Jennifer – she had plenty of good ideas on how the bank could improve its almost non-existent marketing – but the thought of standing up and talking to a room full of senior people . . . 'But you are going to have to do it all the time if you get the job,' her partner David, a corporate finance manager in another bank, helpfully told her. 'You've just got to pull yourself together.'

As the day approached, however, Jennifer's nerves grew worse. She wrote out her talk and tried to memorize it word for word. She practised looking calm and relaxed in front of the mirror. She tried to think of good answers to the critical comments she knew were coming. She couldn't sleep at nights for worry.

Finally her doctor prescribed some sleeping pills. They calmed her down but left her feeling a bit dopey at the interviews. She stumbled through the presentation like a bad dream. She didn't get the job, but she has become determined to overcome this obstacle in her career path. How should she fully prepare herself for the next opportunity?

Presentation skills, the ability to do what used to be called public speaking effectively, are necessary for any manager today. They embrace not only presentations within the organization – such as presenting a possible innovation in product design to colleagues – but also presentations to customers or clients and at seminars and conferences.

My profession has involved me in giving a great number of presentations to audiences of all sizes in many different countries. 'Are you ever nervous still?' people occasionally ask me. 'Yes,' I reply, 'before certain events of an unusual or demanding kind.' But some moderate nerves are helpful. Heart beating faster, adrenalin flowing, palpitations – all these physical changes are the body's way of preparing itself for an exceptional effort. But nerves do need to be kept moderate. Personally I find that deep breathing in a relaxed and calm way before a presentation is enough to keep me operational. But that only works if I am really confident about the content of my presentation, its appropriateness or relavence to that particular audience, and the quality of my visual aids. Also, I need to have rehearsed my presentation thoroughly. If I am speaking alone I can usually rehearse in my mind, using experience to imagine the scene. But even then I need to make some practical preparations, making sure for example that the equipment works. If others are involved and it's a team presentation, we may need one or two actual rehearsals.

When I met Jennifer Huxley, and she told me the above story, she was about to subject herself to a similar selection procedure in another bank and already felt the old sensations coming back. I told her not to worry about her nervous tension. As I have said, it does raise your energy level. We discussed the content of her presentation, making sure there was a beginning, middle and end, and that the whole would fit into the allotted time of thirty minutes, allowing for fifteen minutes of question and answer and discussion. 'Get the framework of main points in your head,' I suggested, 'and use your overhead projector slides both to fill them out and to serve as your notes. Double-check that your slides are legible and uncluttered. Be clear and keep it as simple as possible. Just be yourself – be your best self – and don't try to act a part. Let your message speak for itself. And last, Jennifer, remember that you have to be a bit like the acrobat on a high wire – you have to smile as well!' She laughed and said she would do her best. This time she got the job – with some especially favourable comments on her presentation skills.

THE CASE OF THE TALKATIVE CHAIRMAN

Nobody worked longer hours than Alistair Jackson of DMKG, one of the largest firms of chartered accountants and management consultants in the world. Much of his time was taken up in meetings, and being a senior partner he was normally in the chair. He was a garrulous, social man who enjoyed long business lunches, and a consummate organizational politician as well. He liked to announce his opinions first, and then talk around subjects, usually with an eye on his status and position in the organization. He hated clock-watching and people who left his meetings early, usually on some flimsy excuse that they had an important client waiting or that they needed to catch the post with an urgent letter. He disliked junior partners who interrupted him in full flight. He firmly believed he was an excellent chairman. 'Like Margaret Thatcher I lead from the front,' he boasted. 'Once, in my early days here, I was sent on a chairing meetings course but I found they had nothing to teach me.'

When DMKG introduced '360 appraisal' (appraisal by colleagues and subordinates as well as one's boss), Alistair Jackson had the shock of his professional life. The head of the company gave him the report. Under 'Communication Skills' it summarized his shortcomings as a chairman as follows:

1 AJ's meetings never begin or end on time. He shows an arrogant disregard for the value of other people's time and also for their professional advice or opinions.
2 He is too fond of the sound of his own voice. He can never say things succinctly. His listening ability is minimal.
3 AJ seldom has a written agenda and never circulates one in advance. His planning is all last-minute, usually on the back of a meeting.
4 No control of the meeting – lets his favourites ramble on and doesn't check topic-jumping.
5 Gives the impression that the political standing of his section and division is the most important aspect, and many of his meetings are concerned with delaying or avoiding decisions which may affect them adversely.

'Rubbish!' replied Alistair Jackson, with some heat. 'I know I have got my enemies, and there is a lot of jealousy about my achievements floating around but someone in your position should know better than to place any weight on what a few malcontents say. After all, I am a very senior partner.' The Chief Executive reached for another piece of paper. 'These views are supported by appraisals from twenty-six of your colleagues and eighty-nine junior partners and managers who have attended your meetings or worked in project teams with you, plus four letters from clients commenting on how unsatisfactory they found meetings with you. And, of course, my own assessment of you in my meetings bears it out. So what are you going to do about it?'

Perhaps few managers touch the abysmal depths of poor chairmanship in the way that Alistair Jackson did. Yet few of us cannot improve as chairmen of meetings.

The word 'chairman' sounds rather formal. It conjures up pictures of formal procedures as in parliamentary committees or statutory bodies, such as general meetings of shareholders or boards of directors or groups of trustees. Now, these formal skills are sometimes appropriate: they define, with some precision, the role you must play in order to meet the legitimate expectations of all concerned. A judge in a law court is a good example of a chairman presiding over business in this quasi-formal way.

But I would rather you thought of yourself (when you are 'in the chair') as *a manager of interpersonal communication*. I know that sounds like a piece of jargon, but it embraces so many more situations than those in which you will find yourself elected or appointed to the chair, together with a set of procedural rules. A team coach at half-time, for example, is a manager of communication; so is the conductor of an orchestra during rehearsals.

Whenever people gather it is natural for them to communicate: a two-way or multi-way conversation develops. In business contexts, that conversation is supposed to be purposeful and effective. That requires skills in both leader and team members (it's a useful analogy to think of those at a meeting as being like a team with complementary knowledge/experience/skills with clear objectives in view). It is your job to lead and manage the discussion so that it achieves the ends set out for that meeting. In Chapter 10 we shall explore in more detail what that requires of you in the leader's or chairman's role.

Before leaving the sad case of Alistair Jackson (you've guessed it – he decided to take early retirement and go into local politics), a brief word about appraisals. Remember that all that colleagues, superiors or subordinates (or husbands or wives, sons or daughters) are doing is giving you their impressions. These are objective in the sense that it is a fact that this person has formed this impression. It is not an objective statement of what or who you really are – only God knows that. But cumulative evidence – a pattern of impressions – should be taken seriously (though not necessarily solemnly). As the Hungarian folk saying goes:

> *When a man says you are a horse, laugh at him.*
> *When two men assert you are a horse, give it some thought.*
> *When three men say you are a horse?*
> *You had better go and buy a saddle for yourself.*

THE CASE OF NETMA LTD

NETMA Ltd (the result of a merger ten years ago between Northern Electric Transmissions and Machine Appliances) is a medium-sized manufacturing company facing difficult times. The company makes electrical machines, switches, adaptors and plugs, employing 750 people on three different sites. New competitors, especially in Taiwan and Malaysia, have reduced their market share from 26 per cent three years ago to 9 per cent today. Product changes, compulsory redundancies, rumours of take-over bids and more downsizing have created an anxious, even fearful atmosphere in the factories and offices. Managers spend most of their time in crisis meetings with their accountants and creditors. The staff are kept in the dark, not deliberately but because there are no internal systems for communication except the noticeboards in the three factories, supplemented by what supervisors can glean from their managers.

One day, Bill Hawkins, who had worked in the faulty goods rejection shop for nine years, brought in the local newspaper and read out an advertisement for part-time staff at NETMA Ltd. 'But there aren't any vacancies,' came a chorus of protests. 'Yes, but don't you see,' said Bill, 'they are going to make us all redundant and hire part-time labour — much cheaper, so they will be able to compete with Taiwan.'

'But they can't do that,' objected the union official, 'it would amount to unfair dismissal. Anyway, I heard a rumour that they have developed a new revolutionary product and that we are going to merge with General Electric. Of course, if only they had listened to our ideas we could have improved our present products. If the Japanese can do it we could have done. If only ... .'

'If only we had some leadership, managers who could communicate with us,' interrupted Bill Hawkins. He got up and wrote in red felt-tip pen on the noticeboard:
NETMA = *Nobody Ever Tells Me Anything.*

He then sat down to a round of cheers and applause.

Communication is the lifeblood of organizations. It is a *business* requirement, not just a matter of good human relations. Without good downward, sideways and upward communication, you won't stay in business long these days. Although I will explain what I mean more fully later (in Chapter 12) let me highlight now two major points:

- It is important to establish proper systems of communication. Too many managers either leave it to chance or only communicate when they have bad news to impart.
- Systems by themselves are not enough. They tend to run down or atrophy. All your managers need to be educated to want to communicate, and trained in how to do it. Systems don't learn.

Remember that inexorable equation: SIZE + GEOGRAPHICAL SPREAD = COMMUNICATION PROBLEMS. If you are running a shop with three employees you shouldn't have to worry too much about communication. But if you are going to become a strategic business leader, like the chief executive of NETMA Ltd, then you have to face up to that problem and take steps to solve it.

Exercise

Congratulations on your recent appointment as the new Chief Executive of NETMA Ltd. It's what in my trade we call a challenge! Please write down your strategy for restoring morale. In particular, list a six-point programme to improving – perhaps I should say transforming – the present level of communication in the company. May I add that as Company Chairman – a new boy too – I am looking forward to working with you and I am confident that you are the right person to turn us into a world leader in our field. Could you let me have your communications programme by next Monday – it really is urgent we get this right.

1	
2	
3	
4	
5	
6	

THE CASE OF THE POOR PERFORMER

Michael Williams works for an educational public service as an educational consultant, specializing in helping secondary schools in the region to become more effective and more efficient. He had a background as a maths teacher before becoming a schools inspector and then moving into the new field of educational consultancy. That part of the service is now about to be privatized, but John Denchley – Michael's manager – expresses doubts about him in the new competitive context. For Michael is a consistently average to poor performer. He is not bad enough to be sacked, but lacks any sparkle. He also has a negative attitude to women. Denchley summons him for a personal professional review.

'You are coming along fine, Michael, it's just that we—' he began, remembering somewhere the rule to praise or encourage first, and then to criticize.

'Great, I am glad you are pleased,' Williams interrupted, 'of course, I do have ten years more experience than anyone else in the unit. Some of them are still wet behind the ears. That Sara Middleman, for example, she really gets up my nose, a raving feminist if ever there was one. Probably a lesbian to boot.' He gave Denchley a knowing look. 'Did you know what she said at Stoking High School last week . . .'

Denchley had been muttering sympathetic noises (he had been told to be a good listener on the counselling course) and part of him believed in non-directive help. But his management responsibilities reasserted themselves.

'The object of this meeting, Michael, is to review your performance in the light of privatization next month. The fact is that the Director of the service thinks you are what he calls a "poor to average performer". What have you to say?'

'What a cheek,' replied Williams. 'I have at least twenty years more experience than him. Anyway, I don't know what he means by "poor" or "average" performance, do you? I am a professional, not a performing animal. We aren't running a supermarket, are we, where everything is measured by cash. By what standards am I being measured?'

'Well,' replied Denchley, 'it's more your attitude. People find you a bit abrasive – not me, of course,' he added hastily, 'and perhaps the clients have commented once or twice that you are not helping them much.'

'Ah, you are thinking of that letter from the head of Lanstead High School – silly bitch, she should never have been appointed. Utter rubbish. I have done more school visits than any other member of the unit. Tell that to the Director. There is nothing – nothing – nothing [he banged on the table for emphasis] poor about my performance as you call it. Of course I am not perfect – that seems to be what you managers want. I am not going to sacrifice my life on the altar of business efficiency, not me. Besides, you said yourself that I am coming along fine. Good morning to you.'

The essence of a good appraisal interview is that both manager and subordinate (I don't like these terms but I cannot think of better ones in this context) should agree on the present level of performance and upon a plan to improve it. The above interview foundered on the rock that neither Denchley nor Williams had a clue about what they were supposed to be talking about. They were meeting because they had been told to meet.

In Chapter 8 I shall practise what I preach and set out fully the objectives and performance standards for a really effective appraisal. Here I shall limit myself to a few general points as I reflect on the case above.

Notice how the interview lacks substance because Denchley cannot speak to data: he has no information about whether or not Williams has met his objectives or targets (were any set and agreed?) nor any reliable data about his performance as measured against any kind of standards or benchmarks. In this vacuum Denchley allows the assumption of Williams (that quantity of school visits is the yardstick) to go unchallenged.

Words such as 'poor' or 'average' remain unfocused or fuzzy in Denchley's mind, again giving Williams an easy release from the necessity for hard thought and self-examination. The quality of communication between the two men reflects this fact that they do not have a common language in which to discuss their work. You can see that Denchley has little or no chance of tackling successfully the problem of Williams's negative attitude to women.

Incidentally, who would you want to sack sooner – Williams or Denchley? Neither, you reply. Both can be improved by better leadership. Well, I will give you the chance to prove your point later in the book.

Any appraisal interview worth the name is going to be a demanding exercise for both parties. If you are conducting the interview the requirement is to be:

- TRUTHFUL
- HELPFUL
- TACTFUL

The difficult part is to be all three at the same time!

EFFECTIVE COMMUNICATION – A PERSONAL CHALLENGE

That protestation of Michael Williams about not being perfect reminded me of a story. A man spent many years looking for the perfect wife. At long last he found her. But there was one remaining difficulty. She was looking for the perfect husband!

Perfection is an ideal. It is good to have ideals; they are one of the windows through which the light of eternity streams into our lives. But they are seldom, if ever, attainable in this here-and-now world of our experience. You will never be a perfect communicator, then, and nor will anyone else. YET EXCELLENCE IS WITHIN YOUR GRASP.

You may indeed have glimpsed yourself in one or more of the six case studies, perhaps with a touch of depression. More positively, you may have already begun work on a personal profile of yourself as a communicator. It is your first sketch map of the mountain you now have to climb. When it comes to the uphill business of self-improvement, you may find with most people that 'an inch is a cinch, a yard is hard'. There are no magic formulas. It's a matter of practising, failing repeatedly and eventually learning. Never give up – effective communication in both professional and personal life is too important to you for any weary collapse into mediocrity.

Before you go forward on that lifelong climb, you can at least reflect that the easy slopes – learning to talk, read and write – are already behind you. Of course they were not easy at the time, but looking back they seem so. Now is the time to revisit your reasons for investing in this book. A quick read on a flight to Paris? Or are you going to take it seriously as a test of all your skills as a communicator? Pin down your aims now.

Exercise

As a result of reading this book I intend to improve my communication skills in the following specific ways:

1	
2	
3	
4	
5	

TOWARDS EXCELLENCE: A PERSONAL CHECKLIST

	Yes	No
Do you now regard effective communication as an essential part of your job. Do you see its relevance for the whole of your life?	❑	❑
Have you achieved perfection as a communicator? (Check with your spouse, life partner and at least three colleagues before ticking the Yes box.)	❑	❑
Have you a reasonably clear idea of your strengths and areas for improvement in communication? If so, have you listed them on a separate sheet of paper?	❑	❑
Have you selected which chapters in this book you wish to work on first in the light of your self-profile?	❑	❑

Would you describe your motivation NOW to become an excellent communicator as:

1 a burning desire ❑
2 a strong flame ❑
3 rather flickering ❑
4 very weak ❑
5 non-existent ❑

KEY POINTS

- Communication only happens if you get in touch with people and remain in contact with them. Social distance, as cultivated by some managers, is counter-productive. Live and work among people as their leader, not their remote boss. He or she who communicates, leads.

- Don't confine communication behind organizational fences. Communication with customers or prospective customers, suppliers and supporters, and the public at large, is vital for the health of your business. Have you ever as a customer been on the wrong end of bad communication? Then you know how much it matters.
- You will not get far in most careers – even ones you create and manage yourself – without being called upon to speak in public or make a presentation. Nerves are natural, and you can learn how to control them. The content of what you say is obviously important but *how* you say it – your presentation skills – can be almost equally important, especially in some contexts.
- The first step towards becoming a manager of communication – one who helps others to communicate effectively with each other to some common end – is usually when you are given the role of discussion leader or chairman. Only one in ten managers, some research indicates, is an excellent chairman of meetings. Are you in that happy minority among your peers?
- Organizations have a nervous system of communication which carries information, ideas and inspiration in varying degrees of effectiveness. It is vital to establish a good system of communication and train all your leader-managers – key terminals in the system – in communication skills.
- Giving and receiving constructive praise and criticism is never going to be easy, given the realities of human nature. But you will never be an effective leader until you can do it.

> *Oh I wish some God would give us the power*
> *to see ourselves as others see us – it would*
> *free us from many mistakes and foolish ideas*
> *English version of Robert Burns's 'To a Louse' (1786)*

3

EFFECTIVE SPEAKING

'Speeches are like babies,' it has been said, 'easy to conceive but hard to deliver.' Certainly speeches are like babies in that they come in all shapes and sizes. They range from informal to formal, extempore or prepared. Consider their variety.

An *address*, for example, is a carefully prepared, formal speech, such as delivered by a distinguished speaker or made on a ceremonial occasion, for example an inaugural or valedictory address. It stresses the fact that an audience is in attendance. A political leader, for instance, makes an annual address to the party conference.

An *oration* is an eloquent address meant to stir up the emotions of a group or mass of people. It treats some important subject in a dignified style and manner, according to the rules of oratory, and is usually delivered on a special occasion, as at a celebration, university degree-giving ceremony or funeral. Lincoln's famous Gettysburg Address is a classic example of such an oration. Since true orators are rare, however, the term *oration* is also sometimes used to describe a pompous speech designed for showy, oratorical effect. A *harangue*, by contrast, is an oration out of control. It is a long, loud, vehement address, appealing to passions or prejudices. It may be an extemporaneous tirade or be carefully contrived. Often it is intended to inflame those to whom it is addressed and to spur them to action. The speeches of Adolf Hitler at the mass rallies in Germany before the Second World War were long, ranting harangues.

Speeches can be roughly sorted into categories by their purpose and content. A *discourse*, for example, is a fairly long, carefully prepared, well-organized speech on a definite subject, whereas a *lecture* is the kind of speech given by a teacher to a class. It is a discourse on a given topic, designed to inform and instruct a group of students or some similar audience. *Lecture* derives from a Latin verb meaning to read. The most effective lectures are not read, but giving a lecture does imply extensive previous preparations, including often the writing down of what is to be said. A *sermon* usually means an instructive religious discourse delivered usually by a clergyman or minister to a congregation. Informally, however, words like *lecture* or *sermon*, even *harangue*, may all suggest any form of didactic moral instruction, including formal reproofs, stern rebukes, lengthy reprimands, or earnest exhortations to duty.

Today, especially in relation to management, another form of address is known as the *presentation*, a method now so common and potentially so important for you that it merits a separate chapter in this book. My first encounter with presentations came in the army, for they emerged from research done during the Second World War on the psychology of instruction. The two distinguishing characteristics of presentations are:

- the extensive use of audio-visual aids
- more than one person is often involved, so that a presentation is a team effort – not unlike a play

Many television programmes are in essence such presentations. In industry and commerce the same format now dominates, especially in the context of sales and marketing to new or potential customers.

In order for you to be effective as a speaker in any or all of these forms of public discourse, however, you do have to apply certain principles. These I would compare to the laws of aerodynamics, but in this field they apply to *the power of communicating or expressing thoughts in spoken words*. That power is sometimes singularly lacking, as the following story shows.

> As the executive management group's discussion dragged on it became more obvious that no one had grasped what Michael Mann, the Managing Director, had meant about what would happen if the company did not improve its quality, customer service and competitiveness. Some took it as a coded message that a takeover or merger was imminent; others interpreted it to mean substantial redundancies would be announced next week. Emotions, fanned by the breezes of uncertainty and anxiety, began to blaze into accusation and counter-accusation. Finally, Michael Mann tried to calm the troubled waters by saying, 'I know that you believe you understand what you think I said, but I am not sure you realize that what you heard is not what I meant.'

The above definition, of course, includes both the formal or set-piece engagements outlined above and the much more informal occasions when you are called upon to stand up and say a few words, or you have to open or close a meeting. It even includes some *conversation* – not social chat but those situations where two or more people speak to each other at some length in a relaxed, informal atmosphere often with some purpose or subject in mind. In some civilizations,

including our own in earlier days, conversation used to be
regarded as an art. People, like Jane Austen's heroines in
fiction or Dr Samuel Johnson in fact, were much admired
for their facility in expressing thought in everyday conversation. They did so with economy, wit and command of the
language. Perhaps one day we shall recover the art of
communication in this most homely and intimate of all its
forms.

Now to work. I suggest that there are six key principles,
but the list is open-ended. Please let me know if you can
add to the list. In order to make them easy to remember, I
have set them out as exhortations or self-commands. They
are what I habitually tell myself to do – not always with
good effect!

BE CLEAR

Clarity is the cardinal principle of power or effectiveness in
both speech and writing. Therefore good communication
begins in the mind. The poet Nicholas Boileau expressed
this truth in 1674:

> *What is conceived well is expressed clearly,*
> *And words to say it will arise with ease.*

Clear thinking issues in a clear utterance: if your thoughts
or ideas are a bit confused, vague or fuzzy, then they will
be that much less easily understood or perceived.

Thus the application of this principle begins a long way
back from the boardroom or executive office, in the struggle
to achieve clarity in the uncertain weather of the mind.
This entails mastering the intellectual skills of analysing,

synthesizing and valuing, which are subjects in a companion book in this series, *Effective Decision Making*.

It should not be supposed, incidentally, that what is clear is automatically true. Someone once said that George Bernard Shaw's head contained a confusion of clear ideas. Be that as it may, truth does not always come purified and translucent, and 'All that glisters is not gold'. Clarity is a mercenary value: it serves well whoever is prepared to pay the price for it. That price includes the willingness to suffer muddle, confusion and ambiguity before the clouds part, the dust settles, and the issue, problem or course of action becomes crystal-clear. If it becomes a matter of communicating to others, the combination of truth and clarity is well-nigh irresistible, certainly so in the long run.

One of the masters of our time in applying the principle of Be Clear was Field Marshal Montgomery. His wartime briefings became a legend to those who heard him. As a boy at St Paul's School I heard Viscount Montgomery when he returned to his old school to describe his D-Day plans. He spoke in the very building he had used during the war as Allied Headquarters, indeed in the same lecture room he and the other generals had used for their final presentations to King George VI and Churchill, and so it was not difficult for a fourteen-year-old boy to capture the 'atmosphere', as Montgomery liked to call it. Above all, his refreshing clarity lingers. Brigadier Essame emphasized it in the following account of Montgomery at work in Ronald Lewin's *Montgomery as a Military Commander* (1971).

He could describe a complex situation with amazing lucidity and sum up a long exercise without the use of a single note. He looked straight into the eyes of the audience when he spoke. He had a remarkable flair for picking out the essence of a problem, and for indicating its solution with startling clarity. It was almost impossible to misunderstand his meaning, however unpalatable it might be.

The principle of Be Clear needs to attack like sulphuric acid the corrosions which discolour the work of arrangement, reasoning and expression in our minds. The arrangement or structure of what you are saying should be clear, so that people know roughly where they are and where they are going. The reasoning should be sharp and clean-cut, without the blurred edges of those who gloss over the issues. Above all, the value dimension of the matter in hand should be clarified, for it is this realm which releases most mud into the pools of thought. Lastly, the principle of lucidity invites us to shun the obscure reference, the clouded remark, the allusion which few will understand, or the word which is fashionable but all too muddy in its meaning.

BE PREPARED

Achieving clarity about your aim, content and plan – be it for a formal presentation or an informal speech – is a key part of preparation.

Most people know the terse Scout motto BE PREPARED.

Of course you cannot be prepared for every contingency in life, except in a general sense of having a certain mental resilience by which you can face situations not necessarily known in advance, but you can be ready for those occasions when you know you have to make a speech of some kind or another. You may have weeks or only a few minutes at your disposal, but the principle of preparation is still applicable.

What manner or degree of preparation you can achieve

will vary considerably but it is useful to distinguish between *general* and *particular*. On the analogy of the portrait painter, most if not all of your training and experience should have equipped you for this hour.

> The famous portrait painter Sir Joshua Reynolds, first President of the Royal Academy, once painted the portrait of a successful iron magnate, a self-made man of immense wealth. Like many rich men he was careful with his money. When he received the invoice for some hundreds of guineas – a great sum in those days – he exploded with anger and walked over to Sir Joshua's studio to complain.
>
> 'You spent no more than twelve hours on my face,' he declared, 'and your assistants did most of the work on the rest of me. Why charge me over six hundred pounds for twelve hours' work? I wouldn't pay my best manager that sum.'
>
> 'You are not paying me for twelve hours, Sir,' replied Reynolds. 'You are paying me for over thirty years in which I learnt with much toil and trouble what to do with my brushes in those twelve hours.'

'All my life has been a preparation for loving you,' wrote G. K. Chesterton to his future wife. In the context of communication that *general preparation* reaches back to your schooldays when you learnt to read and write, to discuss and debate, to put up your hand in the class when you knew the answer, and it embraces all your subsequent learning – usually on the job – of the principles and practice of good communication. This whole book is both a summary of and a contribution to all that general preparation that has already taken place in your life.

Particular preparation covers what soldiers would call the tactics of the situation. For the portrait artist it means such activities as putting primer on the canvas, selecting and arranging the brushes and paints, and making sure that the studio is warm as well as well lit. It may have already included some reflection on the personality or character of the sitter who is coming that day – what music they may like to listen to, what they like to talk about or what refreshments to offer them. The equivalents before any kind of communication are set out below, using the framework of Rudyard Kipling's verse from 'The Elephant Child' in the *Just So Stories* (1902):

> *I keep six honest serving-men*
> *(They taught me all I knew);*
> *Their names are What and Why and When*
> *And How and Where and Who.*

In the table below I have changed their order, but it really doesn't matter which one you take first. They are like six chisels that you need to keep in your mental bag, always sharp and ready for service.

BE PREPARED – SOME GUIDELINES FOR THINKING AHEAD	
KEY QUESTION	**NOTES**
Who?	Who are you going to communicate to? Try to visualize them – an individual, several persons or an audience. What are their interests, presuppositions and values? What do they share in common with others; how are they unique?

BE PREPARED – SOME GUIDELINES FOR THINKING AHEAD (Cont)

KEY QUESTION	NOTES
What?	What do you wish to communicate? One way of answering this question is to ask yourself about the 'success criteria'. How will you know if and when you have successfully communicated what you have in mind?
How?	How can you best convey your message? Language is important here. Choose your words with the audience in mind. Plan a beginning, middle and end. If time and place allow them, consider and prepare some audio-visual aids.
When?	Timing is all important in communication. Develop a sense of timing, so that your contributions are seen and heard as relevant to the issue or matter in hand. There is a time to speak and a time to be silent. 'It is better to be silent than sing a bad tune.'
Where?	What is the physical context of the communication in mind? You may have time to visit the room, for example, and rearrange the furniture. Check for audibility (and visibility if you are using visual aids).

BE PREPARED – SOME GUIDELINES FOR THINKING AHEAD (Cont)	
KEY QUESTION	**NOTES**
Why?	In order to convert hearers into listeners you need to know *why* they should listen to you – and tell them if necessary. What disposes them to listen? That implies that you know yourself why you are seeking to communicate – the value or worth or interest of what you are going to say.

Figure 3.1

Time is often in short supply for preparations, but it is rare to find yourself without even a minute or two to make a plan. Such crisis occasions, I suppose, do have the advantage of revealing the person who is more or less always ready to speak in certain areas if called upon to do so. But the good communicator seeks to avoid these surprises.

One lesson I have learnt the hard way is not to become rigid or inflexible. Having planned your work the natural instinct is to work your plan. The difficulty is that plans imply some picture of what the situation is going to be like – and 'on the day' it might not be like that at all.

Henry Compton was incensed by the prospect of having a motorway extension through the fields next to his garden. He carefully planned and prepared what he was going to say at the public inquiry. He listed ten points why it would damage the natural environment, especially the habitat of a rare spotted African woodpecker which occasionally visits these shores.

Once the planning officers had outlined the proposal and the Chairman threw it open to discussion, he waited an opportunity to jump in with his prepared speech, which he had timed for ten minutes.

'Owing to time pressure most of the contributions now will have to be restricted to three minutes. Mr Compton next.'

Henry rose to his feet and launched into his ten-minute speech. By the time he had reached his third point – it all took longer than he thought – the Chairman interrupted him and he had to sit down. All he had done was to repeat what had already been said. His tenth point and ace trump – the African woodpecker – was left out in the cold.

Very committed to his prepared message, Henry Compton was not delicately attuned to the meeting. Had he been so he would have sensed that the numbers of people wanting to speak in a limited time frame would put a premium on hard-hitting brevity. When faced with the need for a last-minute change of plan, he couldn't cope. And so he lost his opportunity. Remember, as an Israeli general once said, 'A plan is a good basis for changing your mind.'

BE SIMPLE

Avoid giving your listeners undue difficulties. In this context *simple* refers to something that is not complicated or intricate and is therefore capable of being quickly grasped by the mind. It should not be confused with *easy*, which merely points to that which requires little effort to do.

The search for simplicity in thinking is the same as the

search for the essence of a subject, that which is specific to it and not composite or mixed up with other matters. Such a quest demands skills of analysing. We have to dissect, discard, blow and burn before we isolate the essential simplicity of a subject. To *simplify* means to render less intricate or difficult and thus capable of being more easily understood, performed or used.

KEEP IT SIMPLE

Former British Prime Minister Harold Macmillan once related how after his maiden speech in the Commons, his legendary predecessor David Lloyd George – one of the great political orators of the century – asked him to come and see him. Lloyd George complimented Macmillan on his first attempt and then gave him a tip: 'If you are an ordinary Member of Parliament, make only one point in your speech (you can make it in different ways but it should centre on one point). If you are a minister, you may make two. Only if you are a Prime Minister, can you afford to make three points.'

At this point we may fruitfully distinguish between making things simple in that sense and *over-simplification*. To be simple requires a lot of hard work, especially if we have to present a subject which has many complications when studied in detail. But even if the subject is inherently complex we still have the choice to make between presenting its complexities in the simplest possible way, or reflecting the complications in both the arrangement of our talk and the language we employ. The ability to speak simply about difficult subjects – without over-simplification – is one of the marks of an effective speaker. We should certainly not fall into the trap of equating simplicity with being simplistic or superficial. What is simple may have depth, just as sophistication may disguise emptiness.

Exercises

- Can you think of someone in your professional field who has the gift of making complex matters sound simple without talking down or becoming simplistic?
- Choose one aspect of your work which is by universal consent not easy for a lay person to understand. How would you explain it to a group of hunter-gatherer South American Indians through an interpreter?
- List three reasons why professional people sometimes deliberately choose to take an essentially simple subject in their field and make it sound as complicated as possible.

It is important, however, that you should have been aware of all the difficulties and worked your way through the complexities to the heart of the matter, to the essential simplicity of the phenomena. This is as true for the scientist as for the manager. Max Perutz, himself a Nobel Prize-winner in chemistry, once commented on the capability of Professor Sir Lawrence Bragg, Nobel Laureate and pioneer of crystallography, in this respect:

> His mind leaps like a prima ballerina, with perfect ease. What is so unique about it – and this is what made his lectures so marvellous – is the combination of penetrating logic and visual imagery. Many of his successes in crystal structure analysis are due to this power of visualizing the aesthetically and physically most satisfying way of arranging a complicated set of atoms in space and

then having found it, with a triumphant smile, he would prove the
beauty and essential simplicity of the final solution.

Wherever we look we find the same story: good speakers
naturally apply the principle of Be Simple, and it is the less
good ones who lose themselves and their audience in a maze
of complications, real and imagined. Former Chancellor
Willy Brandt of West Germany said of Jean Monnet, the
father of the Common Market: 'He had the ability to put
complicated matters into simple formulae.' Doubtless in
politics simplicity is a sign of statesmanship just as it
accompanies outstanding ability in the arts and sciences.

Apart from content and arrangement the principle of Be
Simple should also be applied to language. Here we have to
fight an endless battle against the thoughtless use of jargon
in public conversation or speeches. But again the price of
freedom from this particular piece of professional tyranny is
the knowledge of the complications and ramifications which
the trade vocabulary, signs and symbols have come to stand
for. Otherwise the talk will be *simpliste*. Perhaps we have to
earn the right to speak simply.

'I'm allowed to use plain English because everybody
knows that I could use mathematical logic if I chose,' wrote
Bertrand Russell in *Portraits from Memory* (1956). 'I suggest
to young professors that their first work be in a jargon only
to be understood by the erudite few. With that behind
them, they can ever after say what they have to say in a
language "understanded" of the people.' His advice applies
equally well to all who have to speak to their fellow men
about technical matters.

In practical matters, where the desired result of communication is action, the more simple the instructions of
plans the more likely people are to remember them and

therefore carry them through. Writing to Lady Hamilton in October 1805 from HMS *Victory* (letter reproduced in *Nelson's Letters*, ed. G. Dawson, J. M. Dent, 1960), Nelson described the reaction of his captains to the strategy he outlined for the impending Battle of Trafalgar:

> I joined the Fleet late on the evening of the 28th but could not communicate with them until the next morning. I believe that my arrival was most welcome, not only to the Commander of the Fleet, but also to every individual in it; and when I came to explain to them the *'Nelson touch'*, it was like an electric shock. Some shed tears, all approved – 'It was new – it was singular – it was simple!' and, from Admirals downwards, it was repeated – 'It must succeed, if ever they will allow us to get at them.'

BE VIVID

Nelson certainly made his battle plan vivid. Oddly enough, he avoided giving speeches or making addresses, which suggests that he was no public speaker. He was, however, a most effective communicator to his captains and crews. He could give even a naval strategy visual impact and dramatic appeal. Could you do the same to next year's marketing plan?

The principle of vividness covers all that goes to make what we say interesting, arresting and attractive. From the Latin verb *vivere*, to live, the word vivid means literally 'full of life'. The characteristics it points to spring from the presence of young kicking life in both the speaker (whatever his age) and the subject: vigorous, active, enthusiastic, energetic, strong, warm, fresh, bright, brilliant and lively. When the subject or content is clear and simple it is already well on the road to becoming vivid, but we may still have to let it come to life.

Thus vividness is not something that can be lightly superimposed when all the other preparatory work is completed. Nor is it the result of giving one's personality full play to express itself, like a fountain playing in the sunlight. All public speaking, however slight the occasion, should be 'truth *through* personality'. It is the truth which we have to vivify or bring to life for the other person, never ourselves. Only then can the speaker produce what the poet Thomas Gray called 'thoughts that breathe, and words that burn'.

The first application of the principle Be Vivid is to be interested in what one is talking about and the persons to whom one is talking – in that order. Interest, one of the forms of life itself, is a magnetic quality which is in people and not in subjects. It is true, of course, that genetic inheritance, family upbringing and education predispose us to being interested in certain subjects or topics rather than others. But these fields are as broad as the plains: people, things, ideas, the past, present or future. Within such expanses there are many camping grounds. Moreover, we share some common or universal traits, and if one human person is genuinely interested in some subject it will be surprising if he can find no one to share his interest.

Interest, however, can be a quiet and unassuming movement of the mind. We may acknowledge it in others, but not be necessarily moved to share it. Not all those who have an interest in what they wish to communicate also possess the gift of kindling interest in an audience. But we all find it hard to resist enthusiasm, which is interest blazing and crackling with happy flames. It is extremely difficult for an enthusiastic speaker to be dull: quite naturally he is applying the principle of Being Vivid.

ON ENTHUSIASM – THE LIFE-GIVER

Enthusiasm consists of a permanent intense delight in what is happening in the life around us at all times, combined with a passionate determination to create something from it, some order, some pattern, some artifacts, with gusto and delight. It means attacking problems, puzzles and obstacles with gumption and with relish.

We can develop this drive in ourselves by consciously looking for the enthralling, the exciting, the enchanting, the emotionally moving in even the most routine or most trivial matters, and applying ourselves to it and with all the vigour of which we are capable. We don't have to display a frenzy of histrionics and so become a menace to our friends. But we do need to enjoy unashamedly and uninhibitedly whatever we are doing.

John Casson, 'Are You Getting Through?',
Industrial Society, November 1970

Beyond these essentials quite how you apply the principle of vividness depends upon your creative imagination. Where mass communications are involved, a theatrical sense for the 'drama' may be the way forward. Montgomery and Nelson both 'stage-managed' their communications. 'Monty', alone on the stage, tiers of coloured medal ribbons on his battledress, could communicate the inherent drama of battle. Nor was it perhaps just chance that Nelson loved a former actress, or that he insisted on donning his dress uniform of blue laced with gold on the fateful day of Trafalgar. Above all, he had the ability to capture a great moment and let it speak for itself, with all the flair of a great actor on the stage.

In smaller gatherings or groups and in less intrinsically dramatic situations the attempt to be dramatic can soon land us on the rocks of amateur theatricals. Thus the first step is always to look for *relevant* vividness in the subject. For example, I recall one afternoon's instruction in the army on digging trenches. After a talk on the theory of it, we recruits were marched to the middle of a large field, given spades and told that in thirty minutes a machine-gun would sweep the field with fire. None of us had ever dug so fast in our lives . . . It was a lesson on a fairly humdrum subject, but the instructor had discovered and released the vividness within it.

One way to heighten speech or give it more dramatic impact is to use the colouring of metaphor or analogy. But remember that language should serve meaning, as method should serve content. For both meaning and content are always constantly in danger of 'take-over' bids from language and methods, such as metaphors or visual aids. The test is always the practical one: do people get the message or do they only chuckle over the vivid analogy or colourful visual aid, the illustrative story or the memorable phrase? Demosthenes, by acclaim the greatest of Athenian orators and a prominent political leader in the long struggle against the encroachments of King Philip of Macedon, once said to a rival: 'You make the audience say, "How well he speaks!" I make them say, "Let us march against Philip!"'

Pictures bring vividness, be they actual or verbal. The visual metaphor or simile is a short and vivid picture, which also aids clarity and simplicity. Humour can also enliven working communications, for laughter and boredom cannot live long together. Communication is a serious business, but it need rarely be a solemn one. But the vividness of image or humour, to reiterate the point, should be such as not to draw attention away from the message.

BE NATURAL

To a large extent the previous four principles can be applied before a talk or speech begins, even though there are only a few minutes to consider what you are going to say and how you will put it. The principle of Be Natural, however, belongs primarily to the stage of delivery: it governs our manner of speaking. Of course it can also influence all our preliminary thinking, for both the subject and the methods chosen should be natural to you, or have become so.

EFFORTLESS GRACE

Many things – such as loving, going to sleep or behaving unaffectedly – are done worst when we try hardest to do them.
C. S. Lewis, *Studies in Medieval and Renaissance Literature*

When it comes to public speaking, art (like all grace) should not destroy nature but perfect it. Here situational influences can be especially troublesome. We all know how difficult it can be to act naturally in certain circumstances. We should think nothing of jumping a four-foot-wide stream, but a similar gap several thousand feet up on a mountain cliff can make us freeze with nerves. The principle of Be Natural invites you to shut off the danger signals from the situation, and speak as naturally as if you were standing in your own room at home. Easier said than done.

Yet the art of relaxing can help to fight off the strained voice. The natural and relaxed manners of experienced television entertainers give us plenty of models for observation.

The principle of naturalness is not, however, a licence to be your own worst self before a captive audience. Relaxation can so easily slip into sloppiness, just as 'doing what comes naturally' may be sometimes rightly interpreted by the audience as an inconsiderate lack of adequate preparation. Nor should friendly mumbling or inconsequential chatter, laced with 'you knows', be mistaken for naturalness. The principles must be taken together. Speaking distinctly is the principle of Be Clear applied to the actual activity of speaking: it is our ordinary natural speech magnified to meet the larger situation.

Many of the textbooks on communication devote much space to the techniques of breathing, intonation, pronunci-ation and gesturing. Doubtless there is much to be learnt here, but it is possible to overstress the importance of these elocutionary actions. Beyond the essentials of clear and distinct speech there is little that must be said. Variety in tone and pitch stem from one's natural interest and enthu-siasm. If they are 'put on' or practised in front of the mirror, the result can seem self-conscious and even theatrical – in a word, unnatural. For self-training purposes, however, I have included in Appendix 1 a digest of the advice of one specialist on the use of the voice.

Being natural should not be equated with vocal relax-ation. It includes giving expression in our speech to the natural emotions that human flesh is heir to. Our education and culture teach us to suppress any public display of emotion, and this can make communication sound stilted and artificial. It is unfashionable for orators to weep in public nowadays, although Churchill brushed the odd tear from his eye on more than one occasion. But naturalness follows if we allow the emotions of the moment – interest, curiosity, anger or passion – to colour our voices and movements. Yet they should serve the voice and not master it. 'I act best when my heart is warm and my head cool,' declared the actor Joseph Jefferson, a sound principle for anyone who speaks to an audience.

BE CONCISE

If clarity, simplicity and vividness describe the *quality* of what you say, and truth, beauty and goodness determine the *value* of what you say, conciseness is about the *quantity* dimension. Essentially conciseness means brevity of expression. In an age conscious of the value of time – time is money, as Benjamin Franklin said – and of time management, long-windedness is a short-cut to losing the interest of colleagues as well as customers or clients.

Your ability to confine weighty matters to a relatively small space and time calls for almost surgical skills of thought. As the Arab proverb says, 'Measure the cloth seven times before you cut your coat.' The Latin verb 'to cut' lies behind *concise* just as it gives us *scissors* and *incision* as well. You have to cut out all that is superfluous or elaborative. Aim at the ideal of using exactly as many words as are required to express what you have in mind – and no more.

Exercise

Select a verse from three different poems in your national anthology and write them out or print them on your computer. Now see if you can find any words that are surplus to requirement. If so, delete them even if it affects the rhythm of the poem.

Now repeat the exercise with one paragraph chosen from each of three stories in this morning's newspapers.

Sometimes you will be given a time limit for a particular piece of public speaking. If not, I suggest that you impose one on yourself. Why? Because you do not want to waste time – your own or other people's. Therefore show that you respect the worth of other people's time by being as concise as you can on all occasions when you speak.

Denise Truman was disappointed when Middlewich County Council did not renew her contract to run time management courses. She thought the first three had gone well. Moreover, as a new independent training consultant with a child to support and no partner, she could not afford to lose the business. So she asked to see David Softwell, the director of management development.

'Looking through the evaluation forms, Denise, there is one common theme – you talk too much. People like what you say, but you go on too long. On four occasions, for instance, when you told them that meetings should begin and end on time, your sessions ran over time which meant that the lunch hour was reduced by half.'

It would help Denise – and perhaps you – to think of whatever you have to say in terms of the concentric circle of priority:

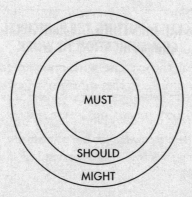

Figure 3.2 Speaking priorities

Must	The core of what you have to say and it has first call on the time available.
Should	Important but secondary. Depending on time it can come into what you say or into any subsequent discussion. Some of it can be left out.
Might	More peripheral material. If time is short it can either be left out or conveyed by the written word.

Every virtue has its darker shadow. Conciseness is no exception. If you are not careful your brevity may come over as terseness to the point of seeming rude, indifferent or mysterious. Incidentally, laconic comes from the Greek name for a Spartan, a people with a reputation for being sparing of words. Avoid the kind of terseness which appears insensitive. For courtesy is the salt in all good communication.

CHECKLIST: PUTTING THE PRINCIPLES OF COMMUNICATION TO WORK

	Yes	No
'You win the match before you run onto the field.' Do you believe this sporting maxim applies to speaking?	❑	❑
Do you take time to plan what you are going to say before and during meetings, interviews and telephone calls?	❑	❑
Has anyone found anything you have said or written in the last week to be lacking in clarity?	❑	❑
Have you taken steps to become a clear thinker?	❑	❑

Which of these statements better describes you:
❑ 'He/she has a gift for making the complicated sound simple.'
❑ 'He/she tends to turn even the simplest matter into something that is difficult and complicated.'

	Yes	No
Are you an enthusiastic, interesting and lively speaker? (Tick No box if the following words have been used about you, or anything you have said or written, in the last year: *dull, boring, lifeless, lacking creative spark, monotonous, flat* or *pedestrian*.)	❑	❑
Do you find it difficult to relax and be yourself when you are communicating?	❑	❑
Have you a reputation for making concise oral contributions and writing succinct letters or memos?	❑	❑
Do you find that you are beginning to enjoy the art of communication?	❑	❑

KEY POINTS

- Speaking takes many different forms, ranging from the formal – addresses, discourses, orations, lectures, homilies, sermons, presentations – to the less formal. The six principles apply to them all: govern the art or power of communicating or expressing thought through the spoken word. Apply them and you will become an effective speaker.

- BE CLEAR makes your communication unclouded or transparent. A clear sky is one free of clouds, mists and haze. With reference to speech it means freed from any confusion and hence easy to understand. Being clear is not primarily a matter of sentences and words. The value of clarity is an inner one: it should act as a principle, purifying thought at its source, in the mind.

- BE PREPARED means active, conscious deliberation and effort before action. To be unprepared, by contrast, means that you have not thought or made any attempt at readying yourself for what you know you may or will have to face. You are like a soccer team that never trains or plans before its matches.

- BE SIMPLE, so that your hearers are not put off by the unnecessarily complicated or intricate. But don't over-simplify or talk down to your audience – even if they are children.

- BE VIVID – make it come alive! This graphic or colour quality springs from the interest and enthusiasm in the mind and heart of the communicator. But it has to become visible in your language.

- BE NATURAL or, if you prefer it, be yourself. What you say and how you say it should reflect your own innate character. For good communication is truth through personality.

- Last but not least, BE CONCISE. Confine what you have to say in a relatively short space, cutting out all unnecessary wordiness. Use words sparingly like bullets, for one accurate shot is worth a hundred misses.

Speak properly, and in as few words as you can, but always plainly; for the end of speech is not ostentation, but to be understood.

William Penn

4

BETTER LISTENING

The objective of this chapter is to help you to become a better listener. Listening has been variously called the neglected art or the forgotten skill in communication. It was in my mind a few years ago to write a book on it and I remember the reaction of a business publisher. 'Listening? No, no. That's "motherhood" stuff. Everyone thinks listening is a good thing, but it confers no benefits. Our best-sellers all have clear and direct benefits to the reader or their business. Look at our titles – they are all practical, how to do it manuals with a bottom line pay off.'

Well, I suppose I must have listened to him in the sense of heeding his advice, because I never wrote that book. Now I have to take my own medicine to Be Concise and condense what is known about the skills of effective listening into one chapter.

THE PHILOSOPHER'S ANSWER

Epictetus, a Greek slave at Rome in the first century, eventually acquired his freedom and began to teach philosophy to those attracted to him.

'Epictetus, I have often come desiring to hear you speak, and you have never given me an answer; now if possible, I entreat you, say something to me.'

'Is there, do you think,' replied Epictetus, 'an *art* of speaking as of other things, if it is to be done skilfully and with profit to the hearer?'

'Yes.'

'And are all profited by what they hear, or only some among them? So that it seems there is an art of listening as well as of speaking . . . To make a statue needs skill: to view a statue aright needs skill also.'

From *The Golden Sayings of Epictetus*, ed. H. Crossley (1909)

It's almost odd to describe listening as a skill. That suggests to me a set of techniques that can be learnt or acquired. There are a few techniques, but they are relatively unimportant. To listen means to hear with thoughtful attention. It is to pay heed to the speaker and to what he or she is saying: careful, alert, watchful and mindful. If you think that sounds easy, remember the Turkish proverb: 'Listening requires more intelligence than speaking.'

If you want to become a better listener, it follows, you may have to review radically your whole approach to life and other people. Is it worth it? Perhaps I should take a leaf out of that publisher's book and start with the benefits.

THE BENEFITS OF BEING A BETTER LISTENER

What desirable good does this comparatively rare ability to listen give you? How does it promote your well-being? As the key to your motivation to improve may lie in giving you reasons for so doing, let me underline some of the advantages.

Listening is a principal way of learning

As inventor and entrepreneur Sir Clive Sinclair says, 'There are bucketfuls of ideas lying around.' What is lacking is listening ears and, it must be added, the entrepreneurial skills needed to bring these ideas to market. Listen for ideas and new information!

PORTRAIT OF A TYCOON – LORD ROY THOMSON OF FLEET

His ability to concentrate was formidable. He would bend the better eye closely upon the sheets of some set of accounts, seven inches from his face, and peer into the heart of a business: generally one he contemplated buying. Figures and statistics were his main, but by no means his sole, guide to a business performance. A very nimble-witted Scottish accountant said that he had never met anyone who could sum a column of figures faster than he could himself until he met Roy. Moreover, he never forgot facts and figures. He seemed to know more about figures than accountants, just as he seemed to know more about law than lawyers . . . To all that poured into the pin-holes of his narrowed vision there was to be added a verbal agility of wit and response. He was not one of your silent tycoons, hearing words and feeling no requirement to acknowledge them. Nobody ever spoke to him without getting not only an answer but a supplementary, a development of the theme, and perhaps some well-timed jocularity as well.

In the same way, he was never interviewed by anyone who could match him in the eliciting of information. His interest was in the hope that the companion might add information to some current concern, or even reveal some world which Roy had not so far entered. One of the best-known women journalists in the United States spent some fascinated hours with him, and said: 'You can say I found him disarming in his simplicity . . . I was totally unprepared for his childlike curiosity about everything. He is full of questions on every imaginable subject. He pumps everyone dry which is enormously flattering. Small wonder he knows something about everything.'

Commemorative article by the editor of *The Times*,
one of the papers owned by Roy Thomson

We take in information and ideas mainly through two organs: our eyes and our ears. In reading these words at the moment you are exercising the first of these two faculties.

Books, papers and screens which you can read or scan seems at first to be a far superior method to receiving information or ideas than listening:

- A listener is often one among others, but when you read a book you do so on your own.
- You can turn back a page or two and re-read; it is often inconvenient or impossible to ask speakers to repeat themselves.

But there are advantages that go with receiving information or ideas through listening as opposed to reading. A knowledgeable talker, for example, will often select facts in order to condense and consolidate their information as they speak, in an effort to give you the essence of it. Writers of books, alas, are not always so economical.

Most people, as they talk, learn from the feedback of their listeners' reactions and modify their spoken words accordingly. A talker, for example, may repeat or rephrase what he or she is saying if you as the listener or the audience look puzzled. That kind of flexibility is not so easily established between a writer and a reader.

Despite what I said above about the practical difficulties of asking speakers, lecturers or broadcasters to repeat a point, in one-to-one conversations or meetings of small groups you usually do have the opportunity for on-the-spot questions of clarification. Readers seldom have opportunities to question writers.

Lastly, through listening we can often obtain information that is not written down. There may have been no time to do so, or the person concerned may lack the motivation and skill to commit what they know to paper.

'Every person is my superior in some way,' wrote Emerson, 'in that I learn from him or her.' Each person you meet is a potential teacher, if only you can find out what they have to teach. Nor will they charge you a fee. Even a bore can teach you something – patience.

Always keep a pocket-book or some paper at hand so that you can take some notes of any new ideas or information. The master thinker knows that ideas are elusive and often quickly forgotten, so he pins them down with pencil and paper. Heed the Chinese proverb: 'The strongest memory is weaker than the palest ink.'

Listening is a way of helping people

Listening to others for ideas and information is self-interested. Almost everyone has some sort of information that can be useful or relevant to you, perhaps at some later time if not now. As for ideas – especially new ideas or seminal thoughts – several hundred oysters may yield only one small lustrous white pearl, but if you don't open the shells will you ever find that pearl?

There is, however, a more disinterested dimension to listening, which is to see it as a means of helping others. Professional helpers – counsellors, doctors, psychiatrists and consultants – are well aware of the human need for someone to listen, especially in those times of stress, anxiety, transition or perplexity which come upon us all as life unfolds.

In such situations we may want information or advice, but more basically we need someone who will simply listen and understand as we talk about things. In today's world there is an increasing tendency to call in the professionals, but such non-directive listening is the office of a friend, colleague or neighbour. Without too much effort on your part, you can do more good in this way.

But, you may say, such listening is very time-consuming. Yes, it is. I am not recommending that you write blank cheques on your time for every passer-by who hijacks your attention with their problems. You may or may not be their Good Samaritan. Remember, however, that here as in so many other areas it is *quality* of listening that matters more than *quantity*. Some research suggests that if you half-listen to someone's problems they will keep coming back for more. Therefore improving your capability as a listener may actually save time for both you and the other person.

Never underestimate the good you can do by simply listening. As Elton Mayo wrote: 'One friend, one person who is truly understanding, who takes the trouble to listen to us as we consider our problems, can change our whole outlook on the world.'

By listening you create a listener

There is a strong tendency to reciprocity or equivalence of exchange among people. You tend to receive what you give, and to give what you receive. If you give listening you may receive listening. If you talk you get talk back.

Now, I know that this principle seems to contradict the complementary nature of human intercourse. If a man treats you as a man should, the proper response is to treat him as a woman should. The natural response to a good speaker is to listen. It's more like a party game where you take turns. If you take the part of listening while the other speaks they are much more likely to take a turn of listening while you speak *with the same thoughtful attention that you have demonstrated*.

'I will teach your ears to listen to me with more heed,' says one of Shakespeare's characters. In planning this book I did consider putting this chapter before the preceding one on speaking. That may seem like putting the cart before the horse. Oral communication – the ability to speak well – tops the lists of essential or desirable management competencies, and listening skills are seldom mentioned. But, if you think about it, the first requirement in a speaker is *that they should create a listener*. There is an analogy here with a business: if you cannot create and keep customers you will soon have no business. Therefore learning about listening ought logically to precede speaking.

The importance of creating a listener or an audience – not assuming them – can hardly be overstated. Musicians will tell you, for example, that the quality of listening can vary from evening to evening, and that an audience who listens well can draw from the orchestra an exceptional performance. As one who earns some of his living by public speaking, I can vouch for that fact from experience. One of our greatest parliamentary orators, William Pitt the younger, once said that 'Eloquence is in the assembly, not in the speaker.'

So much for the benefits that improving your powers as a listener may bring to you. How do you do it? The first step, paradoxically, is to become more aware of what constitutes *poor* listening – in yourself as well as others.

THE DISEASE OF NOT LISTENING

People often confuse listening with hearing. But 'I hear what you say' is not the same as 'I am listening to you.' The latter implies more than reception of sounds, more even than reception of the message. It suggests that thoughtful attention and openness to the implications of what is being said that we have already been exploring. Shakespeare in *Henry IV* makes the difference clear in a courtroom dialogue between that incorrigible old rogue Falstaff and the Lord Chief Justice:

LORD CHIEF JUSTICE: You hear not what I say to you.
FALSTAFF: Very well, my Lord, very well; rather an't please you, it is the disease of not listening, the malady of not marking, that I am troubled withal.

Many of us, like Falstaff, suffer from 'the disease of not listening'. All too often listening is regarded negatively as what you do while you are awaiting your turn to talk. Here are some of the symptoms in the syndrome of poor listening.

Selective listening

Selective listening should not be confused with listening in waves of attention, which is in fact a characteristic of the good listener. Selective listening means that you are pro- grammed to turn a deaf ear to certain topics or themes. Adolf Hitler achieved a unique mastery in this field: he only wanted to hear good news. Those who brought him bad news, or told him the truth, encountered a glassy look and personal insult, if not worse.

The danger in selective listening is that it can become habitual and unconscious: we become totally unaware that we only want to listen to certain people or a limited range of ego-boosting news, or that we are filtering and straining information. But our friends and colleagues know fully well. And they start pre-digesting the material for us, omitting vital pieces and garnishing the rest with half- truths. And in the corridors they may mutter, 'You can't tell him the truth – he doesn't want to know.'

Your mind is like a parachute – it functions best when open.

Persistent interrupting

Persistent interrupting is the most obvious badge of the bad listener. Of course interrupting is an inevitable part of everyday conversation, springing from the fact that we can think faster than the other person can talk. So the listener can often accurately guess the end of a sentence or remark. The nuisance interrupter, however, either gets it wrong or else – even worse – he or she elbows in with a remark which shoots out the fact that they have not been listening to the half-completed capsule of meaning. They may often be working on their own next piece of talk, and therefore be literally too busy to listen. Once the remark is ready, or even half-fitted, they let fly and start winding up for the next one.

Remember that even a fish would not be caught if he learned to keep his mouth shut.

Day-dreaming

Day-dreaming may be a natural escape from an intolerable situation, but it can also be a symptom of poor listening. It is difficult to think two things at the same time. The day-dreamer has 'switched off', and his attention is given to an inner television screen. Some inner agenda has gained precedence over what is being said to him. The poor listener always has a monkey on his mental shoulder. There is a disconnected chatter going into his left inner ear – that holiday, what Mr Jones said, did I switch my car lights off, if only I was managing director I would . . . Emotions can project colour pictures on the inner screen and turn up the sound. Then – farewell to listening.

Succumbing to external distractions

Uncomfortable chairs, noise, heat or cold, sunlight or gloom: the situation can master the listener and drown the speaker and the content. The good listener will try to deal with the distraction in some helpful way; the poor one allows it to dominate their minds and rob them of attention. The higher the quality of listening the less power externals will be allowed to disrupt communication. Listening affirms or builds the relationship in the teeth of forces at work to disintegrate it. The weak listener has no extra reserves to call upon to counter such trying circumstances.

Evading the difficult or technical

Such is our addiction to the clear, simple and vivid that none of us cares for the difficult, long and dull, and we throw the sponge in too soon. We have a low tolerance for anything which even threatens to be difficult, coupled with an impatience at the inability of the speaker to save our time and energy by applying the principles of good speaking. But what is at issue is not merely his or her ability as a speaker but our skill as listeners. If the path has to be tortuous and uphill, the courageous listener will follow. The fainthearted or lazy listener gives up at the first obstacle.

Criticizing the speaker's delivery or visual aids

In set-piece situations such as presentations, lectures or addresses, one way of expressing one's non-listening ability is to fasten on the speaker's delivery or the quality of their audio-visual aids. Some trick of pronunciation, an accent or impediment, involuntary movements or mannerisms: all these can be seized upon as excuses for not listening to the meaning. Or the audio-visual aids, which like Hannibal's elephants can be a terror to their own side, can go on rampage and distract a weak listener. It is hard to listen when the delivery is bad and the audio-visual aids are threatening to get out of control, but such occasions do sort out the hearers from the listeners.

Are you ready for your listening health check?

CHECKLIST: ARE YOU A BORN LISTENER YET?

	Yes	No
Do you pay close attention when others are talking?	❏	❏
When sitting next to someone you don't know at a meal do you always seek to find an area of common interest?	❏	❏

CHECKLIST: ARE YOU A BORN LISTENER YET? (Cont)

	Yes	No
Do you believe that everyone has something to teach or share with you that has value for you – now or in the future?	☐	☐
Can you set aside such factors as a person's personality, voice or delivery in order to find out what he or she knows?	☐	☐
Are you a curious person, interested in people, ideas and things?	☐	☐
Do you respond with a smile or nod or word of encouragement as the speaker is talking? Do you maintain good eye contact?	☐	☐
Do you take notes?	☐	☐
Do you have a good awareness of your own prejudices, blindspots and assumptions, and are you aware that they can create problems for you as a listener? Do you control them?	☐	☐
Are you patient with people who have difficulty in expressing themselves?	☐	☐
'The trouble with you is that you don't listen.' How many times has that been said about you?	☐	☐

- Never   ☐
- Once   ☐
- Occasionally ☐
- Frequently   ☐

	Yes	No
Do you keep an open mind regarding the points of view of others?	☐	☐

CHECKLIST: ARE YOU A BORN LISTENER YET? (Cont)

	Yes	No
Do you listen for the speaker's emotional meaning as well as the subject matter content?	❏	❏
Do you often reflect, restate or paraphrase what the speaker has said in order to make sure you have the correct meaning?	❏	❏

THE SKILLS OF LISTENING

'The fact that people are born with two eyes and two ears, but only one tongue', wrote the Marquise de Sévigné, 'suggests they ought to look and listen twice as much as they speak.' Persuading you to fall in love with listening, turning from the negative to the positive, from symptoms of disease to signs of fitness, I have summarized in the table below the five skills of a good – or very good – listener. You should be able to recognize occasions when you have performed or experienced them all, so it's more a question of widening and deepening your range rather than learning something new from scratch.

Be willing to listen	The will to listening – wanting to listen – comes first. In most contexts listening also requires an openness of mind, a willingness in principle to think or act differently.
Hear the message	Receiving clearly what is actually being said – not a penny more, not a penny less – is the next vital ingredient. There may be problems in physically hearing: if so they have to be overcome. The issue at this stage is not whether or not you agree, but do you hear clearly what is being said?
Interpret the meaning	The meaning in question is the speaker's meaning. It may be clear and intelligible. The test is whether or not you can play back to the other person what they mean in your own words in such a way that they accept it as accurate.
Evaluate carefully	You may want to suspend judgement so that you can use information or ideas for creative thinking purposes. But at some stage or other you will need to assess the worth or value of the content of what you have listened to. Is it true? Is it useful?

Respond appropriately	Communication is two-way. A response is called for. It may be no more than applause – or even silence. But it is still a response, which will in turn be interpreted by the speaker. Make sure you respond appropriately (see page 29 for the distinction between *response* and *effect*).

Figure 4.1 *Summary of listening skills*

In almost all instances of listening some element of *evaluation* comes in. Even if you are given a direct order, for example, by someone with the authority to issue such orders to you, there is still a moment when you must decide whether or not to obey. If there is a moral principle at stake you may decide not to do it. If you are a soldier you may be ordered to shoot an unarmed prisoner, but you ought to refuse to do so. Such occasions are mercifully rare, but the sequence of *evaluation* and *response* is happening all the time. Having grasped someone's meaning you have to assess its degree of truth. You may agree or disagree with the speaker, for example, and that will invariably influence your response.

Active listening is quite hard mental work. Brace yourself to:

- ASK QUESTIONS 'He who is afraid of asking is ashamed of learning,' says a Danish proverb.

Ask not only information-seeking questions but reflective ones as well, such as:

'Would it be true to say that you believe . . .?'

'If you had to sum up your message in one or two sentences, what would they be?'

- **WEIGH THE EVIDENCE**

  Assertions that such and such is the case or is true should always be examined. Some assertions may be self-evident truths, but a rational person requires grounds for accepting others. What grounds for acceptance are being offered? Are they compelling or conclusive?

- **WATCH YOUR ASSUMPTIONS**

  We tend to make conscious or unconscious assumptions. It is difficult to think without making assumptions but the unconscious ones in particular can easily lead us into misinterpreting what the other person is saying. Jumping to conclusions – assuming that we know what someone is going to say or do – is one form it takes. Can you think of others?

You may wonder how you have time for all this critical and creative mental activity when you are busy following the sense of what is being said. A good speaker, of course, will make it easy for you to pay this kind of attention; he or she will also create some time and space for you to think by, for example, not talking too quickly.

CAPITALIZE ON THOUGHT SPEED

Most persons talk at a speed of 125 words per minute. There is good evidence that if thought were measured in words per minute, most of us could think easily at about four times that rate.

The good listener uses his or her thought speed to advantage; they constantly apply their spare thinking time to what is being said. It is not difficult once one has a definite pattern of thought to follow. To develop such a pattern we should:

- Try to anticipate what a person is going to say.
- Mentally summarize what the person has been saying. What point has he made already, if any?
- Weigh the speaker's evidence by mentally questioning it. Ask yourself, 'Am I getting the full picture, or is he or she telling me only what will prove their point?'
- Listen between the lines. The speaker doesn't always put everything that's important into words. The changing tones and volume of his or her voice may have a meaning. So may their facial expressions, the gestures they make with their hands, the movement of their bodies.

Not capitalizing on thought speed is our greatest single handicap. Yet, through listening training, this same differential can readily be converted into our greatest asset.

Ralph G. Nichols, 'How good are you at listening?'
Teamwork in Industry, April 1969

The listener should let the speaker know by verbal and/or non-verbal feedback — occasional words and nods or smiles — that the message is being received and understood. Good listeners make a point of providing such feedback in order to facilitate the communication process. The ultimate test of two-way communication, however, often lies beyond that initial response — the positive or negative. It is to be found in the realm of action: what people actually do as a consequence of the communication, not how they react. Remember that key distinction between *response* and *effect*.

Michael Hewitt nodded enthusiastically. 'Yes, I see what you mean about always being late at handing in work and I get your point about how annoying it is to clients. It won't happen again.' Mark Wilson, the senior partner in the accountancy firm, felt pleased with the way Hewitt's annual performance appraisal had gone. 'At least I have sorted out that problem,' he muttered to himself. 'He really got the message this time.' But had he? Work continued to arrive long after deadlines had expired. Not like Helen, another member of Wilson's team, who had responded so negatively to criticism about her punctuality at the appraisal interview — she even walked out of his office. But — surprise, surprise — her punctuality improved gradually but surely over the next three weeks. Michael or Helen — who had *really* received the message?

ADVANCED LISTENING

Like all arts it is easy to make some improvements, but quite hard to move from SATISFACTORY to GOOD, and even harder to progress from GOOD to VERY GOOD, while EXCELLENT eludes all but those with a special gift and special application. As I cannot claim to be a very good listener myself, all that I can do here is to indicate some of the mountains that remain to be conquered by us.

'It is the heart always that sees, before the head can see,' wrote Thomas Carlyle. A very good listener has to read 'in between the lines'. That means being able to observe and interpret any relevant non-verbal behaviour. The main categories of this undercover language have already been listed in Chapter 1 (page 21) but they need some explanation in this context.

A non-verbal cue, or body language, is a message – often involuntary – conveyed by such things as a speaker's eyes, posture, hand gestures, tone of voice or facial expressions. Use your eyes as well as your ears to take in information. Your unconscious or depth mind works like a computer if you will let it do so, processing all the information that you take in through the gates of the senses. The result may be those richer understandings we call intuitions.

Intuition is a way of knowing that a state exists when there is insufficient evidence for it. The depth mind integrates a number of pieces of data – some absorbed through our senses unconsciously – and forms an intuition which surfaces suddenly or gradually in the surface or conscious mind.

The important rule to apply to intuition is to subject those that come early to the most rigorous and sustained check. If an intuition comes only after acquiring much information or after long experience, coupled with reflection, it is much more likely to be accurate. Early intuitions are often no more than jumping to conclusions. They can be easily fed by our subterranean sources of fear and anxiety.

EMPATHY THROUGH LISTENING

If a conference . . . is to result in the exchange of ideas, we need to pay particular heed to our listening habits . . . Living in a competitive culture, most of us are most of the time chiefly concerned with getting our own views across, and we tend to find other people's speeches a tedious interruption of the flow of our own ideas. Hence, it is necessary to emphasize that listening does not mean simply maintaining a polite silence while you are rehearsing in your mind the speech you are going to make the next time you can grab a conversational opening. Nor does listening mean waiting alertly for the flaws in the other fellow's arguments so that later you can mow him down. Listening means trying to see the problem the way the speaker sees it – which means not sympathy, which is *feeling* for him, but empathy, which is *experiencing with* him. Listening requires entering actively and imaginatively into the other fellow's situation and trying to understand a frame of reference different from your own. This is not always an easy task.

S. I. Hayakawa

Besides insight, or the ability to listen with a third ear as it has been called, the very good or really advanced listener is consistently going to show and use some other qualities or attributes in a rare combination: sensitivity, empathy, patience, humour, curiosity, intelligence, creativity, and – let it be added – endurance. He or she will tend to be a person of wide interests with a natural interest in people. They may be businesslike in listening, but it never shows. For the essence of art is that it makes it seem natural.

Let me conclude with a verse my daughter Kate copied

out and gave me when she was ten years old. It has sat in my file on Listening ever since. Perhaps it was a hint!

> *A wise old owl sat in an oak,*
> *The more he heard, the less he spoke;*
> *The less he spoke, the more he heard.*
> *Why aren't we all like that wise old bird?*

KEY POINTS

- Listening is not the same as hearing. It is the positive business of paying heed or giving your thoughtful attention to someone while they are speaking.
- The benefits of becoming a good listener include information and ideas that could be profitable to you, helping others by lending them your ear, and deepening in the other person the desire to listen to you. 'Listen to him who has four ears,' wrote Zenodotus.
- The first step to self-improvement is to raise your level of awareness of poor or bad listening. The symptoms of the 'disease of not listening' include irrational selectivity, irritating interruption, switching off, mental laziness, succumbing to external distractions, and getting hung up on the speaker's voice or manner.
- Readiness to listen comes first on the list of what you need for this journey. Hearing the message clearly comes next, closely followed by the work of sifting and interpretation. That may lead to further evaluation of its content and import. You should feel responsible for giving some feedback in a conscious way, so the speaker knows if the message has been received and understood. Whether or not

it further engages in your interest, or will later, is another
matter.

- Listening – or at least very good listening – demands the
whole of your mind and heart. That is why the challenge
to become an excellent listener is such an exciting one.
Few of us may become great speakers, but great listening
is within our grasp.

Give us grace to listen well.
John Keble

INTERLUDE

THE CHARGE OF THE LIGHT BRIGADE

A CASE HISTORY OF POOR COMMUNICATION

Theirs not to reason why,
Theirs but to do and die:
Into the valley of Death
Rode the six hundred.

The proverbial schoolboy knows the story of the heroic but useless Charge of the Light Brigade at the Battle of Balaclava: 670 horsemen charged on that fateful afternoon of 25 October 1854; 247 men were killed or wounded and 475 horses slain. The immediate cause of the disaster was the misinterpretation of a written message. But behind that failure, so graphically described in the extract from Cecil Woodham-Smith's book *The Reason Why*, which follows, lay a history of strained relations between those who would have to communicate with each other in action.

You may note down on a piece of paper the specific failures in communication which contributed to the tragic destruction of the Light Brigade.

Lord Lucan (commander of all the cavalry) and Lord Cardigan (the Light Brigade General) had had thirty years of quarrels behind them. More recently Lord Lucan and Captain Nolan (the messenger) had exchanged hot words before Balaclava. And these weak personal links must be set against the general lack of 'team maintenance' or cohesion between staff officers and line commanders, infantry and cavalry, the English and French allies. Thus this glaring instance of bad message writing and passing was but the tip of an iceberg of poor communication; it was upon this cold rock that the Light Brigade foundered.

To appreciate and learn from this disaster it is necessary for the reader to know the essentials of the situation. The Russians in the Crimean War were attempting to intervene in the siege operations before Sebastopol by cutting the British lines of communication to the seaport of Balaclava. The successful charge of the Heavy Brigade and the stubborn defensive resistance of some infantry regiments checked the Russians, but then Lord Raglan, the Allied Commander, spied the enemy attempting to remove some abandoned guns from some high ground to his right. The country is hilly and divided by valleys. Raglan's command post was on the high ground at the head of the long winding North Valley. The Russians occupied the heights on either side of it, and over a mile away, at its other open end, their cavalry was regrouping behind twelve guns. The Light Brigade stood quite near Raglan but almost on the floor of the valley (see map on following page).

Throughout the story it may be helpful for the reader to bear constantly in mind the simple fact that it was the guns on the Causeway Heights that Raglan wished the Light Brigade to secure – not those guarding the Russian cavalry at the end of North Valley. How did Lucan set out towards the wrong objective – and to tragedy? Cecil Woodham-

Smith's account is worth studying closely; it is an unforgettable parable of bad communication:

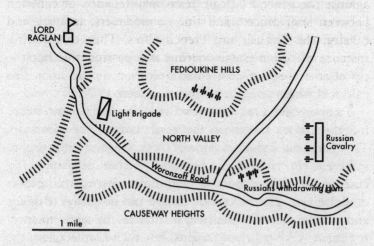

The charge of the Heavy Brigade ended the second period of the battle. The aspect of the action had been entirely changed by Scarlett's feat. There was no longer any question of the Russians penetrating to Balaclava, they had been pushed away from Balaclava, even out of the South Valley altogether, and at the moment their position presented difficulties. They held the Causeway Heights and the redoubts, and they had infantry and artillery on the Fedioukine Hills on the other side of the North Valley, but between them the North Valley, 1000 yards wide, was empty of troops. The troops holding the captured redoubts on the ridge of the Causeway Heights had therefore little support, and Lord Raglan saw that this was the moment to recover the redoubts, the Causeway Heights, and, with the Heights, the Woronzoff Road.

The two divisions of infantry ordered down two hours earlier should now have come into action, but, though the 1st Division under the Duke of Cambridge was present, the 4th Division under Sir George Cathcart lagged behind. He was still in a bad temper, and as he unwillingly left the Heights, General Airey had brought him orders to assault and recapture the redoubts – So! he thought, his division, straight from the trenches and exhausted, was to attack, while the Guards were merely marched in support along the valley below. He refused to hurry.

Lord Raglan's anger was evident; indeed, William Howard Russell noticed that Lord Raglan had lost his usual marble calm and seemed fidgety and uneasy, continually turning his glasses this way and that and conferring with General Airey and General Estcourt. He now sent Lord Lucan a third order, of which two versions exist. The copy which Lord Raglan retained in his possession runs: 'Cavalry to advance and take advantage of any opportunity to recover the Heights. They will be supported by infantry, which have been ordered to advance on two fronts.' The order as it reached Lord Lucan and was retained by him is slightly different. The final sentence is divided into two. After the word 'ordered' there is a full stop and 'advance' is written with a capital 'A', so that the final words read 'They will be supported by the infantry which have been ordered. Advance on two fronts.' The change does not affect the issue. Lord Raglan expected Lucan to understand from the order that he was to advance and recapture the redoubts at once without waiting for infantry support, but that infantry had been ordered, and could be expected later.

Lord Lucan read the order in precisely the opposite sense. He was to advance when supported by infantry. Not only did the words of Lord Raglan's order seem to him to have this meaning, but Raglan's treatment of the cavalry throughout the campaign made it highly improbable that he would order an attack by cavalry alone. Again and again, at the Bulganek, at and after the Alma, on October 7th, the cavalry had been restrained, recalled, forbidden to take the offensive, prohibited from engaging the enemy. Only an hour or so ago Lord Raglan had withdrawn the cavalry from their position at the entrance to Balaclava, where they were preparing to engage the Russian cavalry, and placed them in an inactive position under the Heights. It never crossed Lucan's mind that he was expected to launch an attack by cavalry with the prospect of being supported at some future time by the infantry. He mounted his division, moved the Light Brigade over to a position across the end of the North Valley, drew up the Heavy Brigade on the Woronzoff Road, behind them and on the right, and waited for the infantry, which in his own words 'had not yet arrived'.

Ten minutes, a quarter of an hour, half an hour passed, and the infantry did not appear. Three-quarters of an hour passed, and still Lord Lucan waited. The attack which Lord Raglan wished the cavalry to make appeared to border on recklessness. Redoubt No. 1, on the crown of Canroberts Hill, was inaccessible to horsemen. Nos. 2 and 3 would have to be charged uphill in the face of infantry and artillery. The Heavy Brigade had earlier come within range of the guns in No. 2 and had been forced to retire. However, Lord Raglan, with his power to divine the temper of troops, perceived that the whole Russian Army had bee shaken by the triumphant and audacious charge of the Heavy Brigade and that, threatened again by British cavalry, they would retire. Conversations with Russian officers after the war proved Lord Raglan to be right. A feeling of depression had spread through the Russian Army as they saw their great and, as they believed, unconquerable mass of horse-men break and fly before a handful of the Heavy Brigade. For the moment the British possessed a moral ascendancy, but the moment must be swiftly turned to account, and up on the Heights there were murmurs of impatience and indignation as no further action followed the triumph of the

Heavy Brigade, and down below Lord Lucan and the cavalry continued to sit motionless in their saddles.

Suddenly along the lines of the Causeway Ridge there was activity. Through glasses teams of artillery horses with lasso tackle could be made out; they were coming up to the redoubts, and a buzz of excitement broke out among the staff. 'By Jove! they're going to take away the guns' – the British naval guns with which the redoubts had been armed.

Captured guns were the proof of victory: Lord Raglan would find it difficult to explain away Russian claims to have inflicted a defeat on him if the Russians had not only taken an important position, but captured guns as well. The removal of the guns must be prevented, and, calling General Airey, Lord Raglan gave him rapid instructions. General Airey scribbled an order in pencil on a piece of paper resting on his sabretache and read it to Lord Raglan, who dictated some additional words.

This was the 'fourth order' issued to Lord Lucan on the day of Balaclava – the order which resulted in the Charge of the Light Brigade – and the original still exists. The paper is of poor quality, thin and creased, the lines are hurriedly written in pencil and the flimsy sheet has a curiously insignificant and shabby appearance. The wording of the order runs: 'Lord Raglan wishes the cavalry to advance rapidly to the front – follow the enemy and try to prevent the enemy carrying away the guns. Troop Horse Artillery may accompany. French cavalry is on your left. Immediate. (Sgd.) Airey.'

Captain Thomas Leslie, a member of the family of Leslie of Glaslough, was the next aide-de-camp for duty, and the order had been placed in his hand when Nolan intervened. The honour of carrying the order he claimed was his, by virtue of his superior rank and consummate horsemanship. The only road now available from the Heights to the plain 600 or 700 feet below was little more than a track down the face of a precipice, and speed was of vital importance. Lord Raglan gave way and Nolan, snatching the paper out of Captain Leslie's hand, galloped off. Just as Nolan was about to descend, Lord Raglan called out to him, 'Tell Lord Lucan the cavalry is to attack immediately.' Nolan plunged over the verge of the Heights at breakneck speed.

ANY other horseman would have picked his way with care down that rough, precipitous slope, but Nolan spurred his horse, and up on the Heights the watchers held their breath as, slithering, scrambling, stumbling, he rushed down to the plain.

So far the day had been a terrible one for Edward Nolan; even its sole glory, the charge of the Heavy Brigade, had been gall and wormwood to his soul. He was a light-cavalryman, believing passionately in the superior efficiency of light over heavy horsemen – 'so unwieldy, so encumbered', he had written – and in this, the first cavalry action of the campaign, the light cavalry had done absolutely nothing. Hour after hour, in an agony of impatience, he had watched the Light Cavalry Brigade standing by, motionless, inglorious and, as onlookers had not scrupled to say, shamefully inactive.

For this he furiously blamed Lord Lucan, as he had furiously blamed Lord Lucan on every other occasion when the cavalry had been kept out of action, 'raging', in William Howard Russell's phrase, against him all over the camp. Irish-Italian, excitable, headstrong, recklessly courageous, Nolan was beside himself with irritation and anger as he swooped like an avenging angel from the Heights, bearing the order which would force the man he detested and despised to attack at last.

With a sigh of relief the watchers saw him arrive safely, gallop furiously across the plain and, with his horse trembling, sweating and blown from the wild descent, hand the order to Lord Lucan sitting in the saddle between his two brigades. Lucan opened and read it.

The order appeared to him to be utterly obscure. Lord Raglan and General Airey had forgotten that they were looking down from 600 feet. Not only could they survey the whole action, but the inequalities of the plain disappeared when viewed from above. Lucan from his position could see nothing; inequalities of the ground concealed the activity round the redoubts, no single enemy soldier was in sight; nor had he any picture of the movements of the enemy in his mind's eye, because he had unaccountably neglected to take any steps to acquaint himself with the Russian dispositions. He should, after receiving the third order, have made it his business to make some form of reconnaissance; he should, when he found he could see nothing from his position, have shifted his ground – but he did not.

He read the order 'carefully', with the fussy deliberateness which maddened his staff, while Nolan quivered with impatience at his side. It seemed to Lord Lucan that the order was not only obscure but absurd: artillery was to be attacked by cavalry; infantry support was not mentioned; it was elementary that cavalry charging artillery in such circumstances must be annihilated. In his own account of these fatal moments Lucan says that he 'hesitated and urged the uselessness of such an attack and the dangers attending it'; but Nolan, almost insane with impatience, cut him short and 'in a most authoritative tone' repeated the final message he had been given on the Heights: 'Lord Raglan's orders are that the cavalry are to attack immediately.'

For such a tone to be used by an aide-de-camp to a Lieutenant-General was unheard of; moreover, Lord Lucan was perfectly aware that Nolan detested him and habitually abused him. It would have been asking a very great deal of any man to keep his temper in such circumstances, and Lord Lucan's temper was violent. He could see nothing, 'neither enemy nor guns being in sight', he wrote, nor did he in the least understand what the order meant. It was said later that Lord Raglan intended the third and fourth orders to be read together, and that the instruction in the third order to advance and recover the Heights made it clear that the guns mentioned in the fourth order must be on those Heights. Lord Lucan, however, read the two orders separately. He turned angrily on Nolan, 'Attack, sir? Attack what? What guns, sir?'

The crucial moment had arrived. Nolan threw back his head, and, 'in a most disrespectful and significant manner', flung out his arm and, with a furious gesture, pointed, not to the Causeway Heights and the redoubts with the captured British guns, but to the end of the North Valley, where the Russian cavalry routed by the Heavy Brigade were now established with their guns in front of them. 'There, my lord, is your enemy; there are your guns,' he said, and with those words and that gesture the doom of the Light Brigade was sealed.

What did Nolan mean? It has been maintained that his gesture was merely a taunt, that he had no intention of indicating any direction, and that Lord Lucan, carried away by rage, read a meaning into his out-flung arm which was never there.

The truth will never be known, because a few minutes later Nolan was killed, but his behaviour in that short interval indicates that he did believe the attack was to be down the North Valley and on those guns with which the Russian cavalry routed by the Heavy Brigade had been allowed to retire.

It is not difficult to account for such a mistake. Nolan, the cavalry enthusiast and a cavalry commander of talent, was well aware that a magnificent opportunity had been lost when the Light Brigade failed to pursue after the charge of the Heavies. It was, indeed, the outstanding, the flagrant error of the day, and he must have watched with fury and despair as the routed Russians were suffered to withdraw in safety with the much-desired trophies, their guns. When he received the fourth order he was almost off his head with excitement and impatience, and he misread it. He leapt to the joyful conclusion that at last vengeance was to be taken on those Russians who had been suffered to escape. He had not carried the third order, and read by itself the wording of the fourth was ambiguous. Moreover, Lord Raglan's last words to him, 'Tell Lord Lucan that the cavalry is to attack immediately', were fatally lacking in precision.

And so he plunged down the heights and with a contemptuous gesture, scorning the man who in his opinion was responsible for the wretched mishandling of the cavalry, he pointed down the North Valley. 'There, my lord, is your enemy; there are your guns.'

Lord Lucan felt himself to be in a hideous dilemma. His resentment against Lord Raglan was indescribable; the orders he had received during the battle had been, in his opinion, not only idiotic and ambiguous, but insulting. He had been treated, he wrote later, like a subaltern. He had been peremptorily ordered out of his first position — the excellent position chosen in conjunction with Sir Colin Campbell — consequently after the charge of the Heavies there had been no pursuit. He had received without explanation a vague order to wait for infantry. What infantry? Now came this latest order to take his division and charge to certain death. Throughout the campaign he had had bitter experience of orders from Lord Raglan, and now he foresaw ruin; but he was helpless. The Queen's Regulations laid down that 'all orders sent by aides-de-camp . . . are to be obeyed with the same readiness, as if delivered personally by the general officers to whom such aides are attached'. The Duke of Wellington himself had laid this down. Had Lord Lucan refused to execute an order brought by a member of the Headquarters staff and delivered with every assumption of authority he would, in his own words, have had no choice but 'to blow his brains out'.

Nolan's manner had been so obviously insolent that observers thought he would be placed under arrest. Lord Lucan, however, merely shrugged his shoulders and, turning his back on Nolan, trotted off alone, to where Lord Cardigan was sitting in front of the Light Brigade.

Nolan then rode over to his friend Captain Morris, who was sitting in his saddle in front of the 17th Lancers – the same Captain Morris who had urged Lord Cardigan to pursue earlier in the day – and received permission to ride beside him in the charge.

There was now a pause of several minutes, and it is almost impossible to believe that Nolan, sitting beside his close friend and sympathizer, did not disclose the objective of the charge. If Nolan had believed the attack was to be on the Causeway Heights and the redoubts, he must surely have told Captain Morris. Morris, however, who survived the charge though desperately wounded, believed the attack was to be on the guns at the end of the North Valley.

Meanwhile Lord Lucan, almost for the first time, was speaking directly and personally to Lord Cardigan. Had the two men not detested each other so bitterly, had they been able to examine the order together and discuss its meaning, the Light Brigade might have been saved. Alas, thirty years of hatred could not be bridged; each, however, observed perfect military courtesy. Holding the order in his hand, Lord Lucan informed Lord Cardigan of the contents and ordered him to advance down the North Valley with the Light Brigade, while he himself followed in support with the Heavy Brigade.

Lord Cardigan now took an astonishing step. Much as he hated the man before him, rigid as were his ideas of military etiquette, he remonstrated with his superior officer. Bringing down his sword in salute he said, 'Certainly, sir; but allow me to point out to you that the Russians have a battery in the valley on our front, and batteries and riflemen on both sides.'

Lord Lucan once more shrugged his shoulders. 'I know it,' he said; 'but Lord Raglan will have it. We have no choice but to obey.' Lord Cardigan made no further comment, but saluted again. Lord Lucan then instructed him to 'advance very steadily and keep his men well in hand'. Lord Cardigan saluted once more, wheeled his horse and rode over to his second-in-command, Lord George Paget, remarking aloud to himself as he did so, 'Well, here goes the last of the Brudenells.'

5

THE SKILLS OF WRITING

For most purposes the best form of communication is the spoken word – preferably face to face – backed up by the written word. Say it and then confirm it in writing. Letters and memos that are not follow-ups to oral communication – at a meeting or over the telephone – do demand more skill from you, because they have to do all the vital work of communication and not just a part of it. That brings us to the art of communicating through the written word – writing for short.

You should not suppose that a person who is skilled in speaking will necessarily be a good writer, or vice versa. The spoken and written word perform closely related but different functions. If you have ever read a transcript of a tape-recording of a talk you have given you will see that much revision is needed to render it into readable English. Yet it sounded perfectly all right. Equally, famous writers are often disappointing when they open their mouths.

Being able to set down words in writing gives us two great benefits. First, writing enables us to communicate at a distance, as when you send a letter. In pre-writing days you could, of course, send a messenger, but that was doubtless expensive and also highly unreliable (witness Captain Nolan in the preceding Interlude), as oral messages tend to suffer distortion in transmission. My favourite true story here concerns a prisoner-of-war camp in Italy during the Second World War, where the news that 'The Germans are in Greece' was passed from mouth to mouth and ended up as 'There is going to be a rations increase.'

The second step forward is that writing records preserves knowledge. Previously the only way that information or ideas could be preserved and handed down was by committing them to memory. Poetry and stories (myths, legends, tales, parables) both evolved because they made this labour of memory somewhat easier. The new technology of writing rendered this old technology more or less redundant, just as the introduction of the pocket calculator has made it less necessary for me or you to remember the multiplication tables.

It was no sudden revolution. The Old English word *writan* meant to scratch, draw or inscribe. The story of writing begins with man drawing, scoring or incising various surfaces such as rock faces, dried skins and clay tablets. Its high points include the evolution of alphabets, the emergence of paper and the invention of the printing press. Education as we know it virtually began with the necessity of teaching children – at least the children of well-to-do families – how to read and write while they were impressionable enough to acquire these complex skills. Such children enjoyed a competitive advantage in life over their illiterate fellows. Even today the abilities to read and write are the first rungs on the ladder of formal education, and – still for most people on the face of the earth – the last they will tread.

With difficulty and not by choice you have acquired the basic skill of writing. You could pick up a pen and copy out a sentence or two from this book with ease. Doubtless you write letters to friends or relatives; you may use writing to store information. In this chapter I am assuming that writing is a part of your work, something that you are paid for either directly (as in my case) or indirectly. Now it is relatively unlikely that your trade is to write books (although you may well be interested in writing books or articles for pleasure and profit). But your work will probably include the necessity of writing letters, memos and reports, and possibly more – programmes, courses, scripts, articles – as well.

Communicating on paper is an essential part of any manager's or leader's job, as indeed it is for all of us. For writing effective letters – to customers or clients, to local authorities or public bodies – is part and parcel of effective living. The art of letter writing as a social activity among friends and relatives may have been largely killed by the growth of telephoning as a means of keeping in touch, but the letter for broadly business purposes still flourishes. The advent of the fax machine and the growing use of electronic mail in particular have simply made the exchange of letters or memos much faster.

A letter is a direct or personal written, typed or printed communication, addressed to a person or organization and usually sent by post or messenger. A memo (an abbreviation of memorandum, from the Latin verb *to bring to mind*) is a note to help the memory, a record of events or of observations on a particular subject, especially for future consideration or use. Such information memos in business or organizational life, usually written on paper headed MEMORANDUM, conventionally required no signature but were often initialled by the sender.

Despite the advance of printing and transmission technology the actual business of writing an effective letter or memo comes back to your personal and professional skills as a writer. You may not think of yourself as a professional writer, but if you are in any kind of business, writing letters or memos is *part of your profession*. The aim of this chapter is to help you to become really proficient on paper so that in this respect you are more than equal to the needs of your job.

There are three elements to writing:

- structure and layout
- content
- style and tone

Most of us are taught at school how to lay out a letter and structure it into paragraphs. Report writing is now also taught in the context of project work but it may present difficulties, not least because few teachers know how to write reports (I don't mean the end-of-term ones, though a brushing up of skills there would not come amiss). But it's often the case that beginners overestimate the importance of structure or layout in writing. Usually if you are clear and say what you are doing you can get away with almost anything. Conventions are important, but they are relatively easy to learn and certainly are not the main thing about writing.

Content, by contrast, is literally what it is all about. Obviously I cannot advise you about content, nor can any other textbook on writing. I can help you to cook and present the dish, but the ingredients are yours alone.

How the content of your written communication ultimately fares, however, will depend upon its intrinsic merits or value in that strange marketplace where truth is bought and sold.

In theory it is possible to separate content from form (structure and layout/style and tone), but in practice it is difficult to do so. Therefore you shouldn't think of style and tone as an optional extra, some pink icing on the fruit cake, but as a critical factor in communicating effectively to others. For most intents and purposes, 'the medium is part of the message'.

THE SECRET OF STYLE

Having emphasized the differences between speaking and writing it is now time to look at the other side of the coin. When you write you should think of yourself as talking directly to the person concerned. That is relatively easy if you are writing a love letter but much more difficult if you are writing to people you don't know personally. But it can be done.

Once you start to see writing as a branch of speaking, and not as a separate discipline, you can then apply those six principles which we discussed in Chapter 3. As you will see below, they have emerged not out of my own head but from an evolution of experience in what works in writing English. As early as the seventeenth century, for example, the first historian of the Royal Society, Thomas Spratt, mentioned their rejection of the 'amplifications, digressions and swellings of style' in contemporary writers in favour of a 'close, natural and naked way of speaking'.

ON KEEPING IT SIMPLE

Anyone who wishes to become a good writer should endeavour, before he allows himself to be tempted by the more showy qualities, to be direct, simple, brief, vigorous, and lucid. This general principle may be translated into practical rules in the domain of vocabulary as follows:

- prefer the familiar word to the far-fetched
- prefer the concrete word to the abstract
- prefer the single word to the circumlocution
- prefer the short word to the long
- prefer the Saxon word to the Romance (i.e. Latin)

These rules are given roughly in order of merit; the last is also the least.

H. W. and F. G. Fowler, *The King's English* (1906)

Of course the use of short, concrete words will not in itself do the trick. The principles of clarity and simplicity have to work at the *thinking* level first, and then they may produce the fruit of 'close, natural and naked' language. There are no short cuts to simplicity; because it is an intellectual virtue.

Simplicity is an elusive, almost complex thing. It comes from discipline and organization of thought, intellectual courage – and many other attributes more hard won than by short words and short sentences. For plain talk – honest plain talk – is the reward of simplicity, not the means to it. The distinction may seem slight, but it is tremendously important.

The need for simplicity in language must be balanced against the first principle, which is clarity. All communication, like sketching or painting, involves leaving some things out. The substance and aids to accuracy — stating all the relevant facts, defining terms, following logical steps — demand that certain things should be kept in, even at the expense of brevity. Over-brief or mutilated writing inevitably creates the need for further correcting communications, and so nothing is gained.

The principle should not be seen as separate or detachable guides or rules: they ought to qualify each other like checks and balances in any situation, and it is all of them working together like a team that matters. Be Prepared, for example, ought to include a general knowledge of written English, distilled into such rules as 'prefer the active to the passive verb', as well as the accepted customs over spelling and punctuation. But this should be balanced by the principle Be Natural. The best writers, like the naturally good soldiers of ancient days, are those who have undergone the formal drills and manoeuvres of their discipline, and then been allowed to revert to their former ferocious selves.

THE WINNING COMBINATION

He that will write well in any tongue, must follow this counsel of Aristotle, to speak as the common people do, to think as wise men do; and so should every man understand him, and the judgement of wise men allow him.

Roger Ascham, tutor to Queen Elizabeth I

In today's ever-busier world, where time is at such a premium, the principle of Be Concise is especially important. As a manager, you are dealing explicitly in the commodities of money and time. Long letters or memos cost money in terms of secretarial wages and postal charges. Thus conciseness is an essential for the business writer. Not for you the luxury of spreading yourself over many pages. For a writer, even a letter writer, is drawing upon the precious limited time of the reader, those minutes and hours which measure out our lives. Wasting time is wasting life. Thus, above all, the manager has to aim at an accurate brevity, or at the economy of the reader's or hearer's attention.

In that context of management, letters and reports are the main means of written communication. In the sections below I shall offer you some ideas of how to apply the principles in order to make your products effective.

HOW TO WRITE A GOOD BUSINESS LETTER

As soon as you are more or less clear in your mind what you want to say in the letter, make a first draft on paper or on your word processor if you use one. The golden rule in all writing is to get something on paper or screen and then play about with it.

If possible, I suggest that you leave the letter for some time, so that you come back to it with a fresh and objective mind. Probably you will see at once some things you want to alter. The following table may help:

REVISING YOUR FIRST DRAFT	
KEY AREA	**NOTES**
Objective	The objective or message of the letter should be clear. What response you expect or would like from the reader – if any – should also be clearly expressed.
Order	You may want to revise the order of your points or paragraphs within the broad parameters of BEGINNING, MIDDLE and END.
Style	Check the lengths of your paragraphs and sentences. Try reading the letter out aloud. Take out unintended repetitions. Avoid jargon.
Word selection	Cut out obscure words and clichés, as well as adverbial verbiage like '*by and large, on the whole, all things being equal*'.
Tone	Carry out a tone check on the letter. Is it set in the right musical key? Does the tone accurately reflect your feelings? If necessary, tone down – or tone up.

REVISING YOUR FIRST DRAFT (Cont)	
KEY AREA	NOTES
Grammar/Spelling	Lastly, check the grammar and punctuation. Avoid any spelling mistakes if possible: they may create amusement if not annoyance in the reader, distracting them from your message.
Layout	Does the layout look attractive? Does it sell to the eye?

Figure 5.1   *Steps in letter revision*

Remember to check through and correct the final draft. Then choose the appropriate form of greeting and signature. Ensure that you have attached the relevant enclosures and that you have kept a copy for your file.

THE IMPORTANCE OF TONE

The physical conventions for setting out a business letter need not concern us here. Nor should the common-sense importance for deploying a style that is lucid and clear, so that the reader is left in no doubt as to your meaning, retain us further. But the demand for economy, which I have stressed, can lead to a charge of terseness. It is vital that the *tone* of the letter should reflect your true feelings. The *Oxford English Dictionary* defines *tone* as 'a particular quality, pitch, modulation, or inflection of the voice expressing ... affirmation, interrogation, hesitation, decision, or some feeling or emotion'. Business letters are more likely to be effective if they are written in a tone of courtesy. Watch out for the negative viruses that can so easily infect the tone of your letters.

Curtness	The virus of inordinate brevity communicates unconcern for your reader.
Sarcasm	Most people dislike being on the receiving end of this so-called form of wit, which ridicules by saying the opposite to what you mean.
Peevishness	Includes such whining remarks as 'You ought to know better.'
Anger	The roar of anger, even if it is under your breath, usually provokes an answering roar.
Suspicion	Often takes the form of being suspicious or even cynical about motives.
Insult	Intentional insults are rare, but unintentional ones are not uncommon – especially in replies to applications for jobs.
Accusation	It is obviously difficult to point an accusing finger and maintain courtesy.

Talking down	'In an establishment as large as ours, Miss Smith . . .' The didactic or instructional tone grates in letters, and any teaching has to be done with a light touch.
Presumptuousness	Anyone might be offended by a letter which assumes that he or she will do something before he has made up his mind to do it. The line between confidence and presumption is a fine one.

Figure 5.2 *Some negative elements of tone*

You may feel justified in sending a furious tirade to someone. But there are wiser ways to express your anger, such as a workout in the gym, or digging your garden. You will at least have gained the benefit of exercise. When you have cooled down and begun to write, listen for your still-smouldering embers, like those listed above.

Courtesy is not an 'optional extra' of good style; it belongs to its very heart. Good style shows that you are at least taking the reader's interest seriously. Sir Arthur Quiller-Couch made this point in *The Art of Writing* (1916):

Essentially style resembles good manners. It comes of endeavouring to understand others, of thinking for them rather than yourself – of thinking, that is, with the heart as well as the head . . . So (says Fénelon) . . . 'your words will be fewer and more effectual, and while you make less ado, what you do will be more profitable.'

But what is good manners, as opposed to formal politeness? Courtesy results from a mixture of *cordiality* and *tact*. *Cordiality* being the warmth and friendliness you show towards your reader, and *tact* the sensitivity and discretion with which you choose your words.

CASE STUDY

LINCOLN'S LETTERS TO HOOKER AND GRANT

One of the harder tasks of communication is to express confidence to a person while at the same time rejecting some of his words, actions or policies. Lincoln, a master of direct, simple communication, demonstrated his ability to face and overcome this problem in his letter to 'Fighting Joe' Hooker. Lincoln had considerable difficulty in finding a general up to the standard necessary to beat such Confederate leaders as Robert E. Lee and 'Stonewall' Jackson. By 1863 General Wingfield Scott, the first overall commander, and Generals McClellan and Burnside in the eastern theatre of operations had all retired or been discarded by the President. Despite his careless conversation and insubordinate mien, Hooker had commended himself to Lincoln on account of his offensive spirit. As 1863 unfolded, it became apparent that Hooker was not the man that Lincoln was looking for, but his letter is an eloquent testimony to the President's firm attempt to make the most of Hooker's strengths and to minimize his weaknesses by revealing his knowledge of them and a willingness to discount them for the sake of the common cause.

Executive Mansion
Washington
January 26, 1863

MAJOR GENERAL HOOKER
GENERAL

I have placed you at the head of the Army of the Potomac.
Of course, I have done this upon what appear to me to
be sufficient reasons. And yet I think it best for you to
know that there are some things in regard to which, I
am not quite satisfied with you. I also believe you do
not mix politics with your profession, in which you are
right. You have confidence in yourself, which is a
valuable, if not an indispensable quality. You are
ambitious, which, within reasonable bounds, does good
rather than harm. But I think that during General
Burnside's command of the Army, you have taken counsel
of your ambition, and thwarted him as much as you
could, in which you did a great wrong to the country,
and to a most meritorious and honourable brother officer.
I have heard, in such a way as to believe it, of your
recently saying that both the Army and the Government
needed a Dictator. Of course, it was not *for* this, but in
spite of it, that I have given you the command. Only
those generals who gain successes, can set up dictators.
What I now ask of you is military success, and I will
risk the dictatorship. The government will support you
to the utmost of its ability, which is neither more or
less than it has done and will do for all commanders. I
much fear that the spirit which you have aided to infuse
into the Army, of criticizing their Commander, and
withholding confidence from him, will now turn upon
you. I shall assist you as far as I can, to put it down.

Neither you, nor Napoleon, if he were alive again, could get any good out of an army, while such a spirit prevails in it.

And now, beware of rashness. Beware of rashness, but with energy, and sleepless vigilance, go forward, and give us victories.

Yours very truly,
A. LINCOLN

By 1864 Lincoln had found his man in General Ulysses Grant. Again the President showed his consummate skill as a communicator, expressing the right balance of discretion, encouragement and caution without in any way detracting from the full delegation of executive action. Like its predecessor, this letter illustrates the principles of simplicity and clarity.

Executive Mansion,
Washington,
April 30, 1864

LIEUTENANT GENERAL GRANT

Not expecting to see you again before the Spring campaign opens, I wish to express, in this way, my entire satisfaction with what you have done up to this time, so far as I understand it. The particulars of your plans I neither know or seek to know. You are vigilant and self-reliant; and, pleased with this, I wish not to obtrude any constraints or restraints upon you. While I am very anxious that any great disaster, or capture of our men in great numbers, shall be avoided, I know these points are less likely to escape your attention than they would be mine. If there is anything wanting which is within my power to give, do not fail to let me know it.

And now with a brave army, and a just cause, may God
sustain you.

> Yours very truly,
> A. LINCOLN

WRITING EFFECTIVE REPORTS

The first step is to establish whether the report must stand
alone or serve in a supporting role to oral communication
of some kind – a talk, lecture or a briefing. The latter
might take the form of the presentation of a draft report to
a small committee, followed by another meeting some time
later, when the outline and modifications are explained.
The report then acts more as an *aide-mémoire*. If the situation
allows it, some such combination of oral communication
and report is much to be preferred, especially if some action
is envisaged as a key result.

Your report should begin with an introduction, which
sets out the essential background and crystallizes the aim
and objectives of the report. The latter will have been
already foreshadowed by the title. The format, like a book
in miniature, should include the name of the author and
the date of compilation. The middle body of evidence,
information, issues and discussions should be clearly and
succinctly arranged in a simple order, signposted by chapters, major and minor side headings and numbered paragraphs. The concluding section must leave the reader in no
doubt as to the writer's conclusions and recommendations.

Your key assumptions should be made manifest at the
appropriate places; difficult or technical terms should always
be defined. Illustrations, sharing the characteristics of a
speaker's good visual aids, can save time and space in the

main text, but complicated supporting data should appear as appendices at the end. The minimum requirements for style are not different from those needed for letters or any other forms of business writing. Above all, the report should achieve its stated objective with economy of words, especially where the written word is to be used in alliance with speech.

BREVITY

To do our work we all have to read a mass of papers. Nearly all of them are far too long. This wastes time, while energy has to be spent in looking for essential points.

I ask my colleagues and their staff to see that their reports are shorter.

1. The aim should be reports which set out the main points in a series of short, crisp paragraphs.
2. If a report relies on detailed analysis of some complicated factors or on statistics, these should be set out in an appendix.
3. Often the occasion is best met by submitting not a full report, but a reminder consisting of headings only, which can be expounded orally if needed.
4. Let us have an end to such phrases as these: 'it is also important to bear in mind the following considerations . . . or consideration should be given to the possibility of carrying into effect . . .' Most of these woolly phrases are mere padding, which can be left out altogether, or replaced by a single word. Let us not shrink from using the short expressive phrase, even if it is conversational.

Reports drawn up on the lines I propose may at first seem rough as compared with the flat surface of officialese jargon, but the

> saving in time will be great, while the discipline of setting out the real points concisely will prove an aid to clearer thinking.
>
> Winston Churchill, 9 August 1940

Of course, Churchill's demand for brevity makes for harder work and greater skill. The long-winded and complicated report takes far less effort. Easy reading makes hard writing. Moreover, false marketing doctrine may persuade us that a thick sheaf of paper, pompous prose and unintelligible diagrams may somehow advertise the importance of the subject and the weight of the conclusions.

The requirements and conventions of the written language are indeed different from the spoken one. But you should endeavour to talk to your reader as if he or she is in the same room as you write. Try reading aloud anything you write and see if it sounds like you. Remember that you are not interested (in this context anyway) in writing literary English, nor have you an academic audience in mind. You are writing in order to be understood, and it is you who is writing – no one else. 'Use what language you will,' wrote R. W. Emerson, the American essayist, poet and philosopher, 'you can never say anything but what you are.'

CHECKLIST: WILL YOUR REPORT BE EFFECTIVE?

	Yes	No
STRUCTURE AND LAYOUT		
Is the title page complete and well laid out?	❏	❏
Is the layout clear and easy to follow?	❏	❏
Are any essential parts of the structure missing?	❏	❏
Are the main parts of the structure in the most suitable order for this report?	❏	❏
Do headings stand out?	❏	❏
Is the numbering of paragraphs uniform?	❏	❏
Are the appendices clear and helpful?	❏	❏
CONTENT		
Is the summary of abstract (if included) confined to essentials and a fair statement?	❏	❏

Does the Introduction state clearly: Tick box
- The subject and the purpose of the report? ❏
- The date of the investigation? ❏
- By whom the report was written? ❏
- For whom the report was written? ❏
- The scope of the report? ❏

	Yes	No
Does the main part of the report contain all the necessary facts and no unnecessary information?	❏	❏
Is the order of the main part of the report right?	❏	❏
Is the problem clearly stated?	❏	❏
Does detail obscure the main issue?	❏	❏
Are the sources of facts clear?	❏	❏

CHECKLIST: WILL YOUR REPORT BE EFFECTIVE? (Cont)

	Yes	No
Do conclusions follow logically from the facts and their interpretation?	❏	❏
Are possible solutions abandoned without reason?	❏	❏
Are terms used, abbreviations and symbols suitable and consistent?	❏	❏
Are there any statements whose meaning is not quite clear?	❏	❏
Are facts, figures and calculations accurate?	❏	❏

GENERAL

	Yes	No
Is the report objective?	❏	❏
Are there criticisms which can be made of the report's recommendation?	❏	❏
Is the report efficient and businesslike and likely to create a good impression?	❏	❏
Could a non-technical person directly or indirectly concerned with the report understand it?	❏	❏
Could anyone reasonably take offence at anything in the report?	❏	❏
Is the report positive and constructive?	❏	❏
Does it make clear what decision, if any, is required and by whom?	❏	❏

KEY POINTS

- Clear writing begins in the mind. As Goethe wrote: '*If any man wishes to write in a clear style, let him first be clear in his thoughts.*'
- There are three elements to writing: structure and layout, content and style.
- These can be artificially analysed and dissected, but they should work together as a whole. Structure and layout can be easily learnt. The critical factor in content is the truth of what you say, for truth is the best communicator. But improving your style does take some thought and effort.
- It's helpful to think of writing – letters, memoranda, reports – as talking to someone on paper. Then you can apply to writing those key principles of clarity, planning and preparation, simplicity, vividness, naturalness and conciseness.
- As with all communications, letter and report writing improves in direct ratio to the amount of planning involved. List the major points you want to make in order of importance. Produce a first draft and then play with it until it comes right.
- In speaking, your tone of voice can determine the meaning or import of what you say. Tone is equally present in writing, though harder to get right. It is the musical pitch or vibration in your words which reflects your inner mood or feeling. Make sure – by reading aloud if necessary – that the words in your letter fit the music of your mind.
- Brevity or conciseness is especially important in business or purposeful writing. *I think* is much better than *In my opinion it is considered not an unjustifiable assumption that*. George Bernard Shaw made the definitive comment here

when he handed a letter to a friend by saying, 'I am sorry this letter is so long but I didn't have time to make it short.'

- If this chapter makes it sound easy, remember that writing clearly, simply and understandably is a demanding skill. It takes a lot of hard work to master the art of communicating using the written word – isn't it worth the effort? It's also quite fun.

People think that I can teach them style. What stuff it all is. Have something to say and say it as clearly as you can. That is the only secret of style.

Matthew Arnold

6

THE ART OF READING

''Tis the good reader that makes the good book,' said R. W. Emerson. But what makes a good reader? Reading is the fourth of the major or meta skills of communication. Perhaps more than listening it is the forgotten or neglected one. Few books on communication give it house-room.

One difficulty is that the English language doesn't have separate terms equivalent to *hearing* and *listening* for the written or printed word, and so *reading* covers them both. Reading can be just taking in or comprehending what is on paper or screen. But good reading is listening in action again, giving time and thoughtful attention to what you are reading and remaining alive to all the possibilities it suggests.

TALKING BOOKS

These are not books, lumps of lifeless paper, but *minds* alive on the shelves. From each of them goes out its own voice . . . and just as a touch of the button on our set will fill the room with music, so by taking down one of these volumes and opening it, one can call into range the voice of a man far distant in time and space and hear him speaking to us, mind to mind, heart to heart.

Gilbert Highet

The problems facing the reader who wants a good digestible meal are largely created by the poor culinary skills of the writer. They include:

* poor structure
* unattractive appearance and layout
* turgid and repetitive style
* unnecessary length
* lack of examples or illustrations
* obscure diagrams
* dense or opaque thought processes
* too much information
* too little information
* unpalatable tone

A good reader, in parallel with a good listener, will not be totally fazed by this surface phenomena, especially if he or she feels that gold lies beneath it. Like a gold prospector and digger you may come away with some gold dust or even a nugget, even though the latter may, on later examination, turn out to be fool's gold.

WHAT IS YOUR READING REQUIREMENT?

Before we go any further it is worth asking yourself about the role or part that reading plays in your professional life. For the moment I am setting aside your reading for pleasure or entertainment, not least because you wouldn't be struggling there with the obstacles I have listed above. The novelists or writers of the books you buy or borrow for fun know how to turn you from a hearer into a listener, so that you cannot wait to turn the page and find out what happens next. That is their craft.

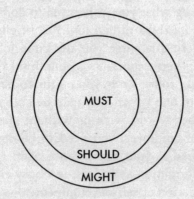

Figure 6   Reading priorities

To help you to clarify your reading requirement go to the core of your job – what are you paid to do. What MUST you read? What SHOULD you read? What MIGHT you read? A consultant neurologist, for example, *must* read certain journals in order to keep up to date. He or she *should* read about developments in related fields, such as the care of long-term patients with spinal injuries. The *might* category covers a wide range of possibilities, but in this instance it could include reading a book on developments in healthcare in Europe or the United States.

Your list will, no doubt, be somewhat similar. Each day on your desk there will be letters, proposals, reports and memos that you *must* read, along with material that falls into the *should* and *might* categories.

Now look again at your job. You are paid, arguably, both to do your job and to improve your job. Does your reading requirement reflect that second dimension? If I may point the question, what have you read in the last six months that has led you to *improve* your existing job as opposed to doing what you were hired to do?

There is also a third dimension. Put briefly, no organization is going to guarantee you the same job for life. We are all on short-term contracts of one kind or another. As well as fulfilling today's role you ought to be preparing for tomorrow's job, one which you may be able only dimly to discern. In other words, with or without the help of your organization or employer, you need to be developing your capability as well as your competence. And reading books, as stores of information and ideas, is a busy element in that process of education or self-development.

If you follow that argument and magnify your reading requirement accordingly, you now face two related problems; not enough time and too much to read. They seem intractable, because you have all the time there is and no one can give you more of it. Nor can anyone stem the spate of publications. There are, however, two possible solutions: learn to read faster and/or become a more selective reader. Each of these merits further exploration.

SPEED READING

Reading is a skill that we learn slowly and with some difficulty. Some people are slowed down even further by a particular brain difficulty, now called dyslexia. Essentially it is a disorder in processing patterns of written or printed words. It is the reading equivalent of deafness or colour blindness. With skilful teaching and determination, these people, who are often very intelligent, can make progress and also learn to cope with their disability. But it is a real handicap.

A child starts to read slowly and aloud because he or she has to make decisions consciously about each word. They begin to speed up when word recognition develops. Pronouncing the word aloud, so that they can distinguish it by the sound, becomes less necessary.

The ability to read silently is the natural climax to the skill of reading, and indeed it is a comparatively recent one. In ancient times it was the practice for the literate few to read aloud, and they were probably unable to read at all without at least audibly mouthing the words. In the fifth century St Augustine of Hippo, while still a young university professor of rhetoric, recorded his admiration for St Ambrose, Bishop of Milan, who he noted – among other things – could read without moving his lips: 'His eye glided over the pages . . . but his voice and tongue were at rest.'

One frequent symptom of a below-average-speed reader is the persistence into adulthood of lip movements or any physical throat tremors, like those of a ventriloquist. One test is to place a finger on your Adam's apple and see if it moves while you are reading silently. For those who do still mouth words a course in reading techniques may prove invaluable.

The average speed an educated person in the West can read without losing full comprehension of the meaning is said to be about 200–250 words per minute, provided the subject matter is reasonably easy – a novel, say. This speed is attained by an averagely intelligent child by about the age of thirteen years; a university graduate will probably average between 300 and 500 words a minute, with some exceptional ones close to 1000 words.

Flashing screens produced by an awesome-sounding

machine called a tachistoscope, blinds which move down the lines of a page, films of print moving at different speeds, carefully graded exercises: these are some of the techniques evolved at Harvard University several decades ago for doubling reading speed. These battery-hen methods made it all look too scientific. The theory was that our eyes move in five or six jerks along a line, pausing while we read in 'fixation'. According to the Speed Reading School the secret is to train the eyes to take in each line in only one or two jerks. The variety of exercises and visual aids mentioned above are designed to induce the reader to adopt this habit.

Personally I do not find this advice very helpful. Once I start getting self-conscious about my eye movements I forget what I am reading about. My suggestion would be to *relax* the eyes muscles, *forget* about eye jerks and let the eyes move *smoothly and evenly* along the line of words, like a scythe regularly sweeping down the long grass.

It is easy to test your speed by roping off a piece of prose and reading it against the clock. But you have to test yourself for comprehension as well. If the material is average in difficulty, e.g. an article in a 'quality' newspaper, you should be able to read it at not less than about 300 words a minute. Arnold Bennett estimated the average book reviewer's speed at eight words per second, which gives 480 words a minute. An Irish professor, doubtless training on Irish whiskey, has claimed 4200 words per minute. If you are much slower, a full reading course, tachistoscope and all, is recommended. Or you may like to try one of the Do-It-Yourself manuals on the subject. But if it is a question of tuning up the engine, all that is needed is some practice. Once our reading habits are set it is hard to change them. And we owe a great deal to those who taught us to read silently, swiftly and with understanding when we were young.

'I am not a speed reader,' said Isaac Asimov, 'I am a speed understander.' Mere physical speed in reading isn't going to help you very much. For at a certain point on the speedometer you will lose understanding and then comprehension.

IN A NUTSHELL

I took a course in speed reading, learning to read straight down the middle of the page, and was able to read *War and Peace* in twenty minutes. It's about Russia.

Woody Allen

Not that there is any special merit in reading slowly, as if that somehow confers more understanding. As Pascal wrote: 'When we read too fast or too slowly, we understand nothing.'

SELECTIVE READING

A second defensive strategy against the growing amount of paperwork is simply to read less of it. In practice that often means sticking to a MUST circle and forgetting about the SHOULD and MIGHT rings of reading requirement. Is there a better way?

Let me review the story in outline. Take a Bible and look at its contents. A Bible, literally a *biblos* or book, is in fact the original library of the ancient Jews. You can see that it contains their whole literature: written-down stories, instruction manuals, chronicles or histories, proverbs and collections of prophecies, all under one cover. The Greeks and even the Romans could have compiled similar libraries of their key books – beginning with Homer – in what we would regard as two or three fat volumes. Erasmus and his generation were the last to be able to read all the books of any significance – the sum of human knowledge – in existence (not, of course, the literatures of China or India or Arabia).

The invention of the printing press brought these libraries – the Bible and the classics – to much wider audiences than the wealthy or learned few who possessed handwritten books. By dint of translating them into vernacular languages, the printers reached even more readers and created a market for yet more books in English, both sacred and secular. The trickle of books and papers became a Victoria Falls of publication. Now no library in the world has space or money to contain let alone keep up with this immense flood of paper, although some – like the Library of Congress – make a valiant effort to do so. Even if such a library existed, your life is too short to do more than nibble at this profusive offering. Putting it all on to computers won't help – you still have to read it.

Not only books but every form of publication has multiplied in response to market forces. Take newspapers. On my shelves I have a copy of one of the earliest newspapers in England, the *Mercuricus Aulicus*. The Royalists printed it in Oxford during the English Civil War. One weekly edition covering all national events is about five A5-sized pages. Compare that to your Sunday newspaper for size! People presumably want quantity and bulk, at a low price, and that is what newspaper proprietors provide. It's odd when you reflect that radio and television have made the news function of the press almost totally redundant.

One possibility is to let others select what you read, always assuming that you have a staff. Very busy people, such as chief executives of companies or heads of government departments, do rely upon trained staffs in this way. The danger, of course, is that they select reading material for you on the wrong criteria, so that you don't get to read what is in your MUST and SHOULD circles of requirement. But this problem is soluble by good communication based on mutual trust, assuming you have both selected and trained your staff carefully to know your mind.

Even the majority of us who do not have staffs can be helped by others to select what we read. Women, for example, rely more on word of mouth than men when it comes to choosing books to read. Personally I operate much the same principle over books on management or leadership, which obviously fall somewhere in my own three circles of reading requirement. If I hear two or three people mentioning a particular book – especially if I respect their judgement – it goes on my list. The selection and advice of specialists – the function of the book reviewer – can also save us much time.

THE SKILL OF SCANNING

So much for the strategy. By some self-managed or delegated process – or perhaps a combination of the two – the piece of writing has now arrived on your desk, be it actual or virtual. As I have said, the written paper may be anything from a fax or letter to a journal or book. Your next tactical step is to *scan* the material in order to judge how much time and attention it needs or merits.

Our word *skill* probably comes from one or two Old

Norse words meaning respectively to distinguish or to decide. The habitual 'decisions' or skill of co-ordinating eye movements with meaning is one aspect of reading. The other skill lies in making accurate judgements in what to read, at what level of thoroughness. For, as Bacon reminds us, 'Some books are to be read only in parts; others to read, but not curiously; and some few to be read wholly, and with diligence and attention.' The skill of changing gear, and adjusting speed to the material, we might call the skill of *scanning*.

Scanning involves the action of quickly glancing down the body of text so that the mind can rapidly take in the gist of what is written. The word *scan* comes from the Latin to climb or leap, so imagine yourself as jumping quickly from stepping stone to stepping stone without getting your feet wet in the text. It should be a wide, sweeping, methodical search, quick but not hasty. *Festine lente*, make haste slowly. Scanning should also be an intensive examination, not a superficial one. It takes time, but it will save you time.

This moving survey from point to point gives you an overall picture. It may lead you to scrutinize parts of the written piece. Scrutiny is another word we took from Latin; it derives from the word for trash or rubbish. So the original scrutiny took place on the rubbish dumps of ancient Rome as the poor sorted out usable rags. It stresses close attention to minute detail. Your thoughtful attention – the essence of good reading as of good listening – has now moved from wide angle to narrow focus:

• prepare by previewing the *content* of the piece which interests you – study the title, sub-headings, illustrations, and writer's aims in writing

- look at the writer's pattern – the structure plan or *method* which he or she has adopted – the table of contents, rough lengths of chapters, appendices and notes
- sample one or two paragraphs to test the writing – density of thought, tone, intelligibility, the 'ring of truth'
- scan (if still interested) the whole or selected parts, looking more closely for the necklace thread of the argument or theme – key paragraphs, sentences or words
- develop actual reading speed with long rhythmic eye sweeps, both horizontal and vertical
- examine more closely the parts or passages which especially interest you, re-reading where necessary

In order to do this more effectively you may have to rid yourself of two rules that tend to be indoctrinated in us from infancy. They are:

- always start at the beginning and read through to the end
- always move your eyes from left to right horizontally over the page (like a typewriter)

Both are good rules for those first learning to read, but they inhibit the person who wants to develop the advanced skill of scanning.

The main danger of scanning is that speed can lead to a gradual loss of control. Like the listener, the reader's first duty is to grasp what the other person means. Depending on the ability of the writer, this can be an easy or near-impossible task. One has to stop and check frequently. Is that what he or she means? What are they really getting at? If one scans too fast it is easy to misjudge a corner and end up in the ditch of culpable ignorance. 'But you *should* have read my letter more carefully . . .' may be the epitaph on your promotion prospects.

We are sometimes inhibited from free perusal or scanning by the second rule: the ingrained sense that *proper* reading means the jerking of the eyes so many times to the right at each line of print. Having freed ourselves from an unthinking adherence to this rule we can develop long rhythmic eye sweeps, zipping vertically down the middle of a page. Additionally we may opt for still less time and employ what the French called *coup d'œil*, the rapid glance that takes in a whole page at a time. Margins help this movement because they act like picture frames. Indeed, it is possible to imagine each page or section as a picture. Individual words are like bricks: it is the message on the wall that matters.

Lastly, you do have to mean business when you are reading. Take a positive but not reverential attitude to the report, article or book in hand. It reminds me of some days when I worked as a deep-sea fisherman. Like a deckhand on an Arctic trawler gutting fish, you have no time to be squeamish. Your knife must go in and slit the book or report down the middle, laying bare that one sentence or paragraph which is the still-beating heart of the written piece. The idea of swiftly and skilfully gutting a book or report may seem repellent, but that is the reality of reading in a world where books, reports or articles fall on our decks in massive shoals.

So we have to rid ourselves once and for all of the idea that the reader has a moral duty to read every word when he takes up a written piece. 'What, have you not read it through?' Boswell once asked. 'No, Sir,' replied Dr Johnson, 'do *you* read books *through*?'

CHECKLIST: READING CAREFULLY

	Yes	No
Are you clear about your purpose in reading any piece of writing with this depth of interest and attention?	❏	❏
Have you some definite questions in mind that you are seeking to answer?	❏	❏
Are they the right questions?	❏	❏
Do you constantly ask yourself questions as you read to stay focused on the subject?	❏	❏
Do you read for main ideas? Can you identify the main idea in each chapter, and the contributing ideas in each section and each paragraph?	❏	❏
Do you critically test the evidence, explanations, examples and other detail offered as grounds for the writer's case?	❏	❏
Have you suitable methods of making notes or recording what you learn or can use?	❏	❏
Do you match or compare the writer's experience with your own? If so, does your experience lend weight to the writer's conclusions?	❏	❏
Is any of it worth reading again (now or later on)?	❏	❏
Shall I discuss the material with anyone? (Who? Why? When? How? What?)	❏	❏

KEY POINTS

- 'What is reading but silent conversation?' asked Walter Savage Landor. The art of reading is akin to the art of listening. Both involve hearing or reading with thoughtful attention, together with a certain economy or grace of effort.

- Writers, like speakers, can pose numerous unintended problems to the reader. A poor or unskilled reader will be thrown by these obstacles, possibly missing the pearl of meaning that lies somewhere within. A good reader, by contrast, overcomes these difficulties.

- What is your requirement? Apart from the priorities (MUST, SHOULD and MIGHT) of your present job and the need to improve the job, add the requirement to develop your potential for tomorrow's tasks. Books and written material play an important part in preparing yourself. What five books, apart from this one, do you plan to work upon in the next twelve months? Remember Mark Twain's words: 'The person who does not read good books has no advantage over the man who can't read them.'

- The explosion of the printed word poses problems. You need to read a lot, your time is limited, and – to make matters worse – there is an ever-growing mountain of information available. There are two possible solutions: to read faster and to select rigorously.

- Speed reading may help, especially if you are naturally a slow reader. But it will not cut down the time bill dramatically. For thoughtful attention and haste cannot sleep in the same bed.

- The principal answer is to be very selective in what you choose to read (beyond the MUST area where you have no choice). Always go for quality rather than quantity. Get the recommendations or professional advice.

- Whatever comes your way by necessity or choice, scan it well first in order to determine at what level you will be reading. Then make the appropriate response, which may be the waste-paper basket or further examination and scrutiny perhaps over several readings, until you have extracted all the juices you need.

- To read without reflecting is like eating without digestion.

Reading is to the mind what exercise is to the body.
English proverb

PART TWO

COMMUNICATION AT WORK

7

PRACTICAL PRESENTATION SKILLS

As I mentioned earlier, my first encounter with presentations was in the army. The military had developed the method out of research into methods of instruction carried out during the Second World War. A presentation, as I have defined already, is a formal or set-piece occasion with two usual hallmarks:

- the use of audio-visual aids
- teamwork

With regard to the latter characteristic, you can give a presentation of your own, but it is more usual to use talk, lecture, address or seminar for such solo efforts.

Not only did presentations play a part in teaching me to become an officer, but later, when I was a civilian senior lecturer in military history at Sandhurst for seven years, one of my responsibilities was to teach the art of presentation to the officer cadets. As part of their obligatory military history course (now renamed war studies) they had to lead or take part in presentations held in the theatre-like college model rooms to their intakes on famous battles or campaigns, such as the D-Day landings. Veterans of these engagements often commented afterwards. My job included giving some further lessons on the battle and then a constructive critique of the presentation skills. The department, I may add, also had to do some presentations as well.

Since those days the practice has now spread into industry and commerce, so that *presentation* has almost taken over from *public speaking* as a general term. Plenty of occasions arise, such as:

- making a marketing or sales proposal
- launching a new product or service
- speaking at a seminar or conference
- running a training session
- presenting your business plan
- ....
- ....

Please add two other examples from your own field. Try to think ahead. If your career plans work out, what sort of occasions for speaking in public will arise?

You can see at once the importance of presentational skills for you. Quite apart from the impact they may have on your business in terms of bottom-line results, presentations are also high-profile events for you personally. To some extent you will be on trial and you will be judged. In some contexts your career or progress may even depend upon your performances.

Therefore your aim should be to develop your presentational skills so that you can present with confidence and effect upon all the occasions that are likely to arise. The actor going on stage is confident that he or she knows the lines and has the professional skills and experience to seize and hold the attention of an audience. Notice, however, the importance here of *context* – the theatre in general, and this particular play or production.

As with all analogies, the comparison between you and an actor will break down at a certain point. You will almost certainly not be mouthing someone else's lines, nor will you be wearing greasepaint or a period costume. More importantly, you are directing and producing your own performance, as well as writing the script and delivery on stage. But the analogy is a strong one, for it suggests to me six main clusters of presentational skill:

- PROFILING THE OCCASION, AUDIENCE AND LOCATION
- PLANNING AND WRITING THE PRESENTATION
- USING VISUAL AIDS
- PREPARING YOUR TALK
- REHEARSING WITH OTHERS
- DELIVERING ON THE DAY

All of these are important, for each contributes to your overall effectiveness as a presenter. You may not be able to control or manage some of the factors – locations, for example – but you should ensure that everything that can be done to ensure success has been done. You will then approach the day with your natural apprehension balanced by a growing confidence and expectation of success.

PROFILING THE OCCASION, AUDIENCE AND LOCATION

When it comes to presentations the first thing you need is to be clear what business you are in, and conversely, what business you are not in. For example, more often than not I turn down requests for after-dinner speeches because I am not in the entertainment business. Nor do I usually accept invitations to speak at sales conferences, for I am not a motivational speaker. Unless you are a genius you cannot take every part in the play. Know the limits of your business, and within it know the limits of your own professional abilities.

Granted that this particular occasion – actual or envisaged – falls squarely within your proper sphere, it follows that you will probably have had some sort of experience of similar occasions. Therefore you will have a rough idea of the audience and you may even have used that particular location before. But as a professional you need to check out all three: occasion, audience and location.

The Nympho Airline was short of cash and hired pilots that other airlines had long since rejected or discarded, such as Captain Nimrod. On his first day he sat down in the cockpit of Nympho's only jumbo jet and balanced his brandy flask on the autopilot unit. 'Let's get going,' he said to the air crew. 'I know all about these jumbo jets. I am an experienced pilot. We are going to Tunisia, aren't we? Been there many times. No, don't confuse me with the route plan or weather forecast – we always get there in the end. Just turn left at Marseilles. Come on, don't waste time checking fuel levels – the ground engineers will have done that. Switch on engines. What is the dinner menu tonight?'

To ensure that you avoid the disasters awaiting the Captain Nimrods of this world and their ilk, I suggest that you work through the checklist below. Its purpose is to bring the event into sharper focus, so that you can shape the most appropriate presentation for it. I have divided the checklist into three sections, but you should always remember to think holistically about presentations. Occasion, audience and location are interactive. I have known one otherwise successful conference virtually ruined by the slowness of service and very low quality of food in the hotel (not booked by me).

CHECKLIST: PROFILING THE OCCASION, AUDIENCE AND LOCATION

	Yes	No
The occasion		
Do you know the aim or objective of the presentation?	❑	❑
Are you clear what kind of occasion it is?	❑	❑
Is there sufficient time for the presentation?	❑	❑
Has time been allowed for discussion?	❑	❑
Do you know who will chair the session and introduce you?	❑	❑
Do they have biographical information about you?	❑	❑
Have you grasped the context – what is happening before and after – of your presentation?	❑	❑
The audience		
Do you know its size?	❑	❑
Can you assess their motivation for being there?	❑	❑

CHECKLIST: PROFILING THE OCCASION, AUDIENCE AND LOCATION (Cont)

	Yes	No
Have you an accurate idea of their expectations?	❑	❑

Is the knowledge level of the audience in relation to your subject:
- ❑ High
- ❑ Mixed
- ❑ Low

Do you know any of them personally or professionally?

All in all, do you expect them to be:
- ❑ Unusually friendly
- ❑ Indifferent
- ❑ Hostile

| Will they be able to use what they hear? | ❑ | ❑ |

The location

Have you a clear picture in your mind of the following:

- ❑ room size?
- ❑ seating arrangements?
- ❑ platform/lectern?
- ❑ acoustics?
- ❑ public address equipment?

- ❑ audio-visual equipment?
- ❑ technical assistance?
- ❑ room temperature?
- ❑ lighting controls?
- ❑ refreshments?

You can sometimes meet your audience in advance if your presentation is part of a series, as at a conference. You can then sense the audience and how they react. It's helpful to think of an audience as not merely a collection of individuals

– although it is that – but as a whole that is more than the sum of its parts, or, in other words, as a social entity that has seen a life and personality of its own.

That assumes, of course, that the audience has been together for some time. If so, you will obviously have an advantage if you can see them in action responding to another speaker or presentation. At least you may learn what not to do! If the audience is assembling just to hear you and your colleagues, remember that they may not know each other (even if they work in the same organization). You will then need to show awareness that they, like yourself, are in a new and perhaps unfamiliar situation. If time and the size of the group allow, it may make sense to encourage the participants to introduce themselves briefly and to outline their expectations.

Locations should always be visited, if possible well before the event. It is all too easy to make *false assumptions* about places. What is a large room to some people is a small one to others. Recently I was invited to conduct a seminar in the presidential suite of an international hotel in an African country. I imagined a palatial set of rooms. In fact I found the twelve participants huddled around the presidential dining table in a room that lacked space for an overhead projector and screen. Always remember the venerable military maxim: 'Time spent on reconnaissance is seldom wasted.' Go and look.

PLANNING AND WRITING THE PRESENTATION

At this point you will need a pen and paper and/or your personal computer. You are now clear about what the occasion is, what is expected of you, who the audience will be and how large it is, and what the location looks like. And, after your negotiations with the organizers, you will also have the limits of the time frame you will share with the audience – the length of time available and at your disposal. Now the real work starts.

What is your objective?

It's good practice to state your objective or objectives at the beginning of your presentation and why you think it is important. Therefore you need to be clear in your own mind about what you are aiming to do and why it is worthwhile.

In this context it's useful to make a distinction between general and specific purpose. Purpose in the general sense can be qualified but not defined. Your general purpose may, for example, be *educational*, *religious*, *political* or *commercial*. It will be implicit if not explicit in the business you are in. Indeed, it is that general purpose which determines the nature of your business, and it will almost certainly underlie your presentation.

Your purpose or objective for the presentation, however, needs to be much more sharply focused. It should have at least some of the following key characteristics of a well-set objective. Tick the box if you have a particular presentation in mind and your objective meets these criteria.

CLEAR	☐	REALISTIC	☐
SPECIFIC	☐	CHALLENGING	☐
MEASURABLE	☐	WORTHWHILE	☐
TIME-BOUNDED	☐	PARTICIPATIVE	☐

Not all of these criteria will be relevant. You may find it hard to MEASURE your effectiveness in achieving your objective in an educational presentation, for example, as opposed to a commercial pitch to prospective customers. Nor will it always be possible to get the audience to PARTICIPATE in agreeing the objective.

The TIME-BOUNDED criterion is especially important. Many presentations fail because the presenter attempts to achieve too much in the time available. If you have only twenty minutes to explain a new lawn-mower product to a convention of garden centre buyers you don't have time to sketch in the whole story of humanity's application of machinery to practical problems, together with a discourse on the evolution of the modern garden. You can CHALLENGE yourself and the audience, but only if you are REALISTIC about what can be done in the time available.

Make a plan
Having written down your objective or objectives, focused at the right level of specificity for the occasion, your next job is to sketch out a framework or skeleton of your presentation. Reduced to the most simple it should have a BEGINNING, MIDDLE and END.

PHASE	NOTES
Beginning	Introduction by chairman. Your introductory remarks. State your objective(s) and give some reasons why they are relevant to the audience. Signpost the main outlines of the presentations.

Middle	Break the complex whole of the presentation down into manageable parts, just as an author divides a book into chapters. Three, four, five or six sections, usually no more. Make sure that you illustrate main points by examples or support them by evidence. A half-time summary is often a good idea, especially if it is a longish and complicated presentation. Put a time estimate against each of these parts or sections and double check that most time goes on top priorities.
End	A summary is often a good way to initiate the last phase. Don't leave your conclusions to chance. Refer back to your objective and prepare your final remarks with that in mind. End on a high note – positive and upbeat.

Figure 7.1 *Planning the presentation*

With planning it's best to take several bites at the cherry. Allow plenty of time for your depth mind or unconscious to work on the problem. For example, I made my first plan for this chapter some months ago, but I have revised it several times since then. For on each occasion I found that I had come to a different conclusion. Of course you do have to draw the line somewhere, bearing in mind that no one ever makes a perfect plan. That is why books are never finished – only abandoned! You are looking for a workable, feasible plan – not a perfect one.

Before you go into production, why not show your plan to the sponsors of the event? Several minds are better than one at this stage of planning. Weigh and consider any constructive comments, then make the necessary amendments, even if it means going back to the drawing board.

USING VISUAL AIDS

'A picture is worth a thousand words,' as the Chinese proverb says. Why? Because we take in much of our information – more than 50 per cent – through the gateway of our eyes. Therefore there is always a strong case for using visual aids, especially if your presentation is primarily about conveying information.

The range of audio-visual aids grows apace. Film, video, CD-ROM, computer-controlled slide, 35mm slide, overhead projector and tape-recorder are only some of the aids available. Although computer technology will gradually replace some of the more traditional aids, the overhead projector and 35mm slide projector, together with the lowly but useful flipchart and felt-tipped pens, will still be with us for some time.

TYPE	PROS	CONS
	Easy to use. Can be used with lights on. Flexible in slide order.	But difficult to use well. Can be jerky and time consuming. Picture often seems distorted.

TYPE	PROS	CONS
	Looks professional. Better with large audiences. With a remote control it is easy to manage yourself.	Requires more dimness, so audience may have difficulty in taking notes. Slide order is inflexible, so not good in interactive situations.
	Easy to prepare. Can look good if carefully prepared. Most informal of aids. Good with a small group.	Difficult to transport. Not readable by large audience. Doesn't look really professional. Takes time to write – with loss of eye contact.
	Tape-recorder can introduce variety – recorded interviews, background music.	Difficult to synchronize. Needs a lot of rehearsal.

Figure 7.2 *Visual aids*

Whether or not you make them yourself on your computer or commission others to make them, remember to apply the principles of CLARITY, SIMPLICITY and VIVID-NESS. The art of slide-making is to know what to leave out. If you are going to give much the same presentation more than once it is highly advisable to get the best professional help available to you in the design and making of your visual aids. If you tell a specialist what you want to communicate, they should be able to help you to encapsulate and support your message on slide.

Some general tips on using visual aids:

- Use a series of overhead or projector slides to structure your presentation for you and allow you to look at the audience whilst developing each point. Look at the audience more than your slides.
- Present only essential information on each slide.
- Restrict the content to about twenty-five words or the equivalent in figures.
- Realize that an ordinary typewriter doesn't look professional and cannot be read at a distance.
- Make sure your slides are clearly numbered in the correct sequence and are the right way up. Any confusion will damage your professional image.
- Use pictures, drawings and colour for interest – 'A picture is worth a thousand words', remember.
- Don't leave any one visual aid on for too long.

Don't imagine that the list in the box above exhausts the possibilities. If you really are trying to sell a lawn-mower at that garden centre convention, why not produce the actual lawn-mower, together with a short video of it demolishing the hay in the back garden? Your product is always your best visual aid in such commercial presentations.

Visual aids are important and I have always had a passion for them. For I prefer to look with my audience at a picture, to share and explore it together. It reflects a fundamental concept about communication. My concept or model of communication is actually more A than B:

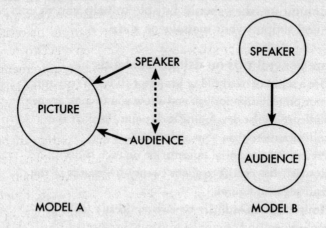

MODEL A   MODEL B

Figure 7.3   *Two models of communication*

PREPARING YOUR TALK

Unless you have a modern and sophisticated autocue system at your disposal, such as prominent politicians use at major conferences, I would counsel against reading from a written script. Doing so certainly has the advantage of greater accuracy, but it loses your eye contact with your audience. An experienced speaker using a written script, like Winston Churchill for example, can glance up frequently and make it sound more natural. But even then the disadvantages outweigh the advantages, especially as we now live in an age which values informality.

When should you read a written presentation? Giving a radio talk is one such occasion, for exact timing matters and you cannot see your audience to make eye contact. Even in the radio studio, however, you will probably find yourself looking up from your script and addressing the invisible audience – actors in radio plays certainly do so.

Perhaps if you have to give a scientific paper or some prestigious lecture which will be published, writing it down and reading it out will be expected of you. Even then it may make more communication sense to give your audience the written paper before or after your presentation and content yourself with presenting it rather than reading it out verbatim. In communication speaking and writing perform different but related or overlapping functions, and it is unwise to confuse them.

At the other end of the spectrum, why not speak without notes? If you are a professional speaker, as I am, you should always do so. It is not such a difficult art to master as you may think. Actors, comedians and concert musicians do not refer to notes, why should you? The practice of doing so leaves you free to look at your audience and to think on your feet. It does take more time in preparation, of course, but it is invariably worth it.

By 'learning the part' I don't mean committing a fully written-out script to memory, as the actor or comedian or musician does before going on stage. You have to memorize the plan – the structure or skeleton of your presentation – together with any facts, quotations, stories or examples. The test is that you must be confident that you can give the presentation without recourse to notes. Your short-term memory is probably much more trustworthy than you imagine. Does it matter if you get the odd word or phrase wrong?

In between the extremes of reading out a prepared script and talking without notes there are several other options. If it is a 'one-off' presentation and if you lack confidence to abandon your notes altogether, you could use your overhead projector/35mm slides or flipcharts as notes. Or you could prepare prompt cards, with a punch hole in the corner and some string to hold them in order and for ease in turning over. Another possibility is to have your presentation outline on a large sheet of paper in front of you on the lectern, but out of sight of the audience.

Whatever method you choose to employ you do need to decide upon it in the planning phase and then work hard like an actor to imprint your presentation within your short-term memory. Even actors have a prompter in the wings should they forget their lines. Keep a copy of your presentation notes on you or near you, so that you can glance at it again on stage. Never be afraid to fish it out and look at it during your presentation if you momentarily lose your bearings.

REHEARSING WITH OTHERS

A rehearsal is a private performance or a practice session prior to a public performance. You may need more than one rehearsal before an important presentation. But you can over-rehearse, which kills spontaneity and therefore offends the principle of Be Natural. A good orchestra will rehearse several times but leave something in reserve to come out on the night of the actual performance.

If you are presenting as part of a team it is essential to have a rehearsal or two, preferably in the place where you will give the presentation. The mutual constructive criticism that follows will lead to improvements. This practice session allows you to tune up your own instrument, going through your part and hearing the sound of your own voice in that particular room. It promotes a smooth and graceful co-ordination of effort among the team. Lastly, it enables you to check out all the equipment and visual aids. (Are they legible from the back row or far corner of the room?)

SETTING THE STAGE

In a theatre, stage management is the organizing or mechanics of effective presentation. It includes setting the stage, lighting it, providing the right properties at the right time and in the right place. The stage manager's job is to manage all these mechanics so that the actor doesn't have to think about them. If anything goes seriously wrong every member of the audience is going to see it and there is no possible way in which the stage manager could explain why it has gone wrong or to justify its going wrong. It had just gone wrong and from that moment it is irretrievable in the minds of the audience. If something happens for which he or she feels the need to apologize, or should apologize, then he or she has failed.

A good stage manager's attitude of mind is therefore at all times one of using his or her imagination to anticipate every conceivable disaster that could or might occur. The stage manager does it by mentally going through every operation that every actor and every member of the stage staff might have to perform, and checks to see that everything has been done to see that the operation can be performed as easily and as safely as possible. It's his or her job to see that nothing happens that will distract actors and audience from their close interaction with each other.

John Casson, 'Are You Getting Through', *Industrial Society*, November 1970

Even if you are speaking on your own and you decide against actual practice sessions (as opposed to mental rehearsals which really are essential), you should always take the earliest opportunity to reconnoitre the place, checking the seating arrangements, lighting and acoustics, potential external or internal distractions, and any equipment which is being supplied for your use. You should not be satisfied until you (or someone you trust) have seen the equipment in question working. In my experience the things that can go wrong with film projectors, tape-recorders, closed-circuit television and overhead projectors are legion. 'I'm sorry, I am not used to this particular model,' hisses the operator apologetically as the machine breaks down.

But it is you as the presenter who carries the responsibility: you will have communicated to your audience that you have failed to observe the first communication principle of Be Prepared. Remember that your audience may well have read this book as well as you! Of course, you will gain marks if you show unflappability, or even fish out the odd spare part from your pocket – but who wants to live dangerously?

DELIVERING ON THE DAY

If you have done your homework you shouldn't encounter any big surprises when you come to give your presentation. There may, however, be some changes 'on the day' that you haven't anticipated and you must make a judgement about making any changes in the content or methods of your presentation. Having done that, you and the audience are ready to go on the journey together. Now all depends on your delivery skills.

PHASE	NOTES AND TIPS
Beginning	If the chairman's introduction needs amendment do it courteously and with thanks. Capture your audience. Explain the background and objectives for the presentation in as concise, clear and vital a way as possible, giving your audience time to tune into your voice and accustom themselves to you as a person. Tell them what you intend to do.
Middle	'Grace, pace and space' – the hallmarks of a good motor car – should characterize your presentation. Keep it moving as you cover with professional ease your prepared points. Let the audience know in advance if you want them to ask clarifying questions as you talk or to save them until after you have finished. Try to sweep the whole audience with your eyes as you speak, so that everyone feels included. Remember to vary the tone of your voice and not to speak too fast or too low. Look pleasant – people like looking at someone who appears to be enjoying himself.
End	Signal to your audience when you are entering this phase. Don't introduce new ideas or information but consolidate what you have done. End with a bang: a short, strong conclusion. Always prepare carefully and learn your last two or three sentences.

PHASE	NOTES AND TIPS (Cont)
Questions/ Discussion	Repeat any questions that may be inaudible to parts of the audience. Try not to be long-winded in answering them. Promote discussion by asking a few questions of your own. Make sure that all the lights are on in this phase. Be courteous always and express appreciation. Disentangle multi-part questions and answer each part separately.
Conclusion	Avoid the session petering out by further summarizing the discussion and reinforcing any action points. Close with some words of thanks.

Figure 7.4   *Speaking skills*

The news that you are going to take part in a presentation is enough to set the alarm bells ringing in most people's minds. No wonder that most people – like Jennifer Huxley in Chapter 2 – are often plagued by nerves before such public exposures. Perhaps you may be one of them. How can you learn to cope with nerves?

CHECKLIST: ARE YOU A NERVOUS SPEAKER?

	Yes	No
Do you ever feel self-conscious if you have to stand up and speak to a group, even if you know them quite well?	❏	❏
Do you experience difficulty in finding the right words to express yourself clearly?	❏	❏
Do you get unpleasant symptoms, such as palpitations, feeling sick, a dry mouth, sweaty palms or breathlessness?	❏	❏
Does your mind ever go completely blank before you stand up to speak?	❏	❏
Do you fear it might and that you will then forget what you were going to say and make a fool of yourself?	❏	❏

As Jennifer Huxley found, there are ways of overcoming nerves. The first step is to realize that nerves are normal, so don't be alarmed by them. Some degrees of nervous tension before a presentation is actually a good thing. It gets the adrenalin flowing and prepares your mind and body for a superlative performance. Some simple relaxation exercises, like deep breathing, can help to keep these pre-event nerves in a manageable state.

Why does it happen? Your body cannot distinguish too well between danger situations. Prompted by your mind, it interprets a public presentation as a danger situation, which arouses anxiety if not fear. Why should it do this? Probably because being watched by a large number of people reminds our primitive selves of being potential victims under observation from hungry predators or enemies lying in wait in an ambush. Our body changes prepare us for fight or flight. If you are wounded in a fight, for example, it's better not to have food in your stomach. So it is natural to feel or be sick on the threshold of perceived danger situations.

You can see that *perception* plays a large part in keeping these natural physical reactions within manageable proportions. No actor could go on stage every night if he or she perceived the audience to be hostile. There are occasionally hostile audiences but on the whole we go to the theatre in a positive frame of mind, wanting to be entertained or enlightened and willing the cast to succeed. Half the battle is to persuade yourself that the audience is on your side, either already or potentially so. Why else would they have come?

When speaking on formal occasions, you can move about if you wish. But the most comfortable anchor stance is to have your feet placed slightly apart and the weight of the body thrown slightly forward on to the balls of the feet. There is then no fidgeting or unnecessary movement. Gestures spring spontaneously from the words which are on your lips.

All movement is potentially expressive of personality. Nervous fidgeting can send the wrong signals. You can learn to control it. Constant smoothing of the hair, a rhythmic rising on the toes, fiddling with markers, pens or glasses, swaying from side to side, pacing to and fro, fastening or unfastening of a button, the jangling of coins or keys in a pocket, all these are merely controllable nervous habits. Do anything you like with your hands but don't have them in the same place the whole time.

Lastly, remember that a presentation is theatre. Act as if you are already in possession of supreme self-confidence. Be a little larger than life and let your enthusiasm show on your face. We are all geese pretending to be swans. Even swans, you remember, may seem to sail with lordly indifference, but underneath they are paddling like hell to keep going. Here are some paddles for you:

Breathe deeply	Breathe well down into your lungs. This enables your diaphragm to control the release of breath from your lungs as you utter each word.
Manage your hands	If your hands seem to 'get in your way', clasp them loosely in front of you, or place them behind your back. Train yourself to forget them.
Look at your audience	Look at your audience all the time you are speaking and embrace them all in your glance. Try to forget yourself in the urge to communicate.
Move well	Let your movements be deliberate and *unhurried*. In a big hall, make them a little larger than life.
Talk slowly	Do not let your rate of utterance exceed your rate of thought. Only so can you avoid the danger of 'stumbling' over your words. In fact, do not think of *words* now – think only of ideas and mind pictures.

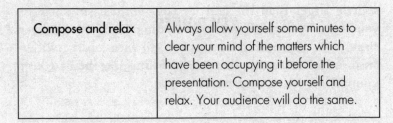

Compose and relax	Always allow yourself some minutes to clear your mind of the matters which have been occupying it before the presentation. Compose yourself and relax. Your audience will do the same.

Figure 7.5   *The six physical steps to confidence*

A good presentation should be like a performance by a world-class orchestra. When you sit back merely to enjoy — not technically to analyse — a piece of music, are you consciously aware of the 'pom-pom, pom-pom' of the trombones, the trill of the flute and so on, as separate components of the work? Are you not rather aware of the entire symphonic effect of the *combination* of sounds?

If a speech pleases, grips, interests, informs — the qualities essential to a speech — it is not because you are conscious of the effect of each of its components. It is because the whole attitude of the speaker combines to produce an *overall* effectiveness. Knowledge, design, narrative, all the arts of good delivery, are combined to make communication effective. As a contemporary said of Demosthenes, 'He that only *hears* Demosthenes loses much the better part of the oration.'

KEY POINTS

- Presentations are addresses to an audience using audio-visual aids and usually involving more than one person working together as a team. You need to be able to take an effective part in a presentation and know how to lead such a team. There are six pillars of success.

- *PROFILING* the occasion, the audience and the location allows you the strength of fore knowledge. To be forewarned is to be forearmed. In this context it is the way to apply the principle of Be Prepared.

- *PLANNING* your presentation, with a structure of general points supported by detail, will give you the framework for success.

- *SELECTING* the right visual aids is a major step towards ensuring that your presentation is going to be effective. Make certain that any visual aids you use are CLEAR, SIMPLE and VIVID.

- *PREPARING* your talk embraces both committing what you are going to say to your short-term memory and preparing any prompt notes. You should aim to talk without notes. Seldom if ever should you read from a script.

- *REHEARSING* is a recipe for success. It builds confidence before the actual performance. Included under this heading is checking out that the 'stage management' aspects of the presentation are all in hand.

- *DELIVERING* the presentation calls upon your effective speaking skills of being clear, simple, vivid and natural. Look after the main ideas and the words will look after themselves. Imagine yourself as leading your audience on an interesting, exciting and potentially fruitful journey.

- 'Fail to prepare; prepare to fail.' The best way to beat nerves is to build your confidence. The foundations for confidence are laid long before your presentation begins but you may still have to act confidently on the day.

A flame should be lighted at the commencement and kept alive with unremitting splendour to the end.

Michael Faraday, Advice to a Lecturer

8

SUCCESSFUL INTERVIEWS

We can define an interview as a meeting, usually between two people, arranged with a clear purpose and with the roles of the participants well defined. The word itself comes from the French verb *s'entrevoir*, to see each other.

Interviews range from a meeting or conversation between a journalist or radio or television presenter and a person whose views are sought for publication or broadcasting, oral examinations of candidates for a job or place in higher education, to an interrogation of a person by the police about a specific event – sometimes euphemistically known as 'helping the police with their inquiries'. What do interviews have in common?

- They are usually prearranged, with the possible exception of the dismissal interview.
- Both interviewer and, generally, interviewee need to prepare for them.
- They all have a definite purpose, which should be clearly known to both participants.
- They all centre upon communication – 'the process by which meanings are exchanged between people through the use of a common set of symbols' (see page 22).

Most managers think that they are good at conducting interviews, just as most of us think we are good drivers. How would you assess your own ability in this respect? In fact interviewing, like driving, is an art with its advanced levels. But you don't have to be ill in order to get better. However proficient at interviewing you may believe yourself to be, there is always room for improvement.

In this chapter, I shall first remind you of some common-sense points, and then move on to discuss structure, the different types of question you can use, and finally, the performance or appraisal interview. My reason for focusing upon the last is that it often poses particular communication problems. Selection interviews, for example, deal mainly with the exchange of information – about the candidate and about the job – which, from the communication point of view, is relatively straightforward. The art of judgement – choosing the right person – of which interviews are merely a part, falls outside the scope of this book, although it is a subject I hope to address later. By contrast, appraisal interviews involve the importing of praise and criticism. This can be much more emotive, and when emotions rush through the door, meaning often jumps out of the window. This type of interview does call for very good communication skills, both on the part of interviewer and the interviewee.

Because of their overtones, the words *praise* and *criticism* are now often being replaced in management jargon by the more user-friendly or neutral-sounding *feedback*. One writer, for example, talks about *affirmative feedback* and *developmental feedback*, presumably praise and criticism. Feedback is a systems term by origin. It refers to a loop in which one part of a system gives information to an antecedent part so that the collective function can be improved. Giving praise and criticism are more than feedback in the strict sense of the partial reversion of the effects of a process to its source, for they are forms of teaching.

This chapter is written with you as a leader or manager in the role of interviewer in mind. But in reality you will often be the interviewee. Use your whole experience and come to understand the skill of interviewing by studying it down both ends of the telescope.

SOME GENERAL ADVICE ON INTERVIEWS

Purpose
The principle of Be Clear requires that you *both* know the purpose of this personal meeting. Are you both clear about it? What else is on the agenda? The first step is to confirm that you share a common mind on that score.

You may well have stated orally and/or in writing what you conceive to be the purpose, but it is usually necessary to check that the interviewee shares your perception. Otherwise you will be talking at cross-purposes.

One way of clarifying purpose is to ask yourself – and perhaps the other person – about outcomes. What are the 'success criteria' for this interview? How will we both know that it has been successful?

Exchange of information
Be clear about what information you are wanting and expecting to receive. Equally, consider what information may be asked of you. If it is a selection interview, for example, you may be asked about pay and conditions if these have not already been communicated. You may be asked about career prospects, leadership development

programmes, the nature and scope of changes in the organization, and so on. Be prepared to give honest and candid answers. Tell people the realities of the situation. Never lure them to work for you under false pretences. Putting it another way, if the information you exchange isn't true or accurate, then you are passing counterfeit notes.

Keeping control

The first responsibility of leadership is to take and keep control. As interviewer, your role is the leading one. You will be expected to guide the discussion.

Keep to the subject in hand and avoid going off in all directions. If the conversation becomes rambling and increasingly irrelevant, you will both lose sight of the aim of the interview.

Bear in mind the purpose of the interview and get to the point early on. This is especially necessary where difficult things have to be said.

Don't talk too much yourself. You are primarily in the listening role. In ordinary conversation the balance between talking and listening is roughly equivalent. But in interviewing you should aim to speak no more than about 20 per cent of the time. Most of your talking, moreover, should be in the form of questions. If you are asked information-seeking questions, confine your answers to what the interviewee needs to know.

Finally, try to stick to the time allocated. The principle of Be Concise should prevent you from overrunning, providing that you have budgeted time correctly for the interview. Interviews ought to be more like sprints than marathons.

STRUCTURING THE INTERVIEW

Structuring or planning the interview is necessary if it is to avoid becoming a shapeless conversation. The amount of structure will depend upon the purpose of the interview and your own experience. The more experienced you are, the less you will need a pre-planned structure of questions to be asked. You should always, however, have a note of the main questions or issues you want to ask or raise.

Like games of chess, interviews have a beginning, middle and end. Each requires skill, as does making the transitions from one to the other.

Opening
- Introduce yourself and any other important factors.
- Confirm the purpose of the meeting straight away.
- Put the other person at ease.
- Try to encourage an atmosphere where both of you are relaxed, open-minded, committed to the purpose and prepared to discuss things calmly and frankly.

Middle
- Keep your aim firmly in mind as you exchange information.
- Keep the discussion relevant, helpful and work-oriented.
- Listen, or give the other person's replies or comments your thoughtful attention.
- Listen to the person as well as what they say, and so listen with your eyes as well as your ears.
- Make sure you have covered the agenda.

Closing
- Sum up the discussion.
- Describe the action you have decided or mutually agreed upon.
- Confirm the worthwhileness of the meeting.
- Avoid ending abruptly.
- Close on a positive, if not a higher, note.

THE SKILL OF ASKING THE RIGHT QUESTION

Questions are the tools of interviewing or — more widely — of listening. The art of interviewing largely consists of asking the right questions at the right time. There are several different kinds of question, each with its pros and cons. It is useful to have them all in your repertoire, so that you don't get stuck like a broken record on only one type of question.

QUESTION	USES	DISADVANTAGES
The Yes/No Question e.g. *'Have you read this report?'*	Good for checking facts. Establishes where a rough balance lies quickly (e.g. 'Are you healthy?')	Can force over-simplified answers (e.g. to the question 'Are you or are you not satisfied with your job?')
The Closed Question e.g. *'How long have you worked here?'*	Best where facts or data are sought. Form of question restricts answer to a limited area	Can sound like an interrogation. Leaves little room for discussion or explanation

QUESTION	USES	DISADVANTAGES
The Open-ended Question e.g. *'How do you see your career progressing?'*	Good for opening up the exchange and discussion of information and ideas	May invite long and rambling answers, leading into irrelevancies
The Leading Question e.g. *'Don't you agree that you should have done that weeks ago?'*	Not very useful, unless you are trying to push someone in a certain direction	The knowledge gained by a leading question is usually limited in value
The Loaded Question e.g. *'What do you think about the chief executive's stupid plan for expansion in Europe?'*	Limited, unless it's deliberately provocative	A loaded question is charged with some hidden implication or underlying suggestion. It has a bias or prejudice built into it. Can blow up in your face
The Prompt e.g. *'So what did you do then?'*	Keeps things moving, guiding the interviewee in content and direction. Clarifies if the other person has not understood what you want	Can prematurely curtail or direct an interesting reply to an open-ended question

QUESTION	USES	DISADVANTAGES
The Probe e.g. '*What precisely was the extent of your budget responsibility in Canada?*'	Obtains more information, following through from the general to the particular	Can make it all sound like an interrogation
The Mirror e.g. '*So you felt completely fed up at this point?*'	A reflective way of checking whether or not you have received the other person's message accurately	Be careful that you do not introduce a slight alteration of meaning: 'No I felt rather frustrated, but not fed up'
The What-if Question e.g. '*Supposing we opened an office in the Gulf, would that interest you?*'	Making assumptions or creating situations imaginatively and asking what the interviewee would do	Can force someone's hand or lead to unfulfilled expectations. Only yields hypothetical information

Figure 8.1   *Types and descriptions of questions*

PERFORMANCE APPRAISAL

The performance appraisal interview has as its main purpose the improvement of an individual's work contribution. As an interview, it is governed by the general principles or rules already explored, and there is nothing to add on that front, except the obvious point that if you haven't set or agreed objectives some months or weeks in advance it is more difficult to hold a successful appraisal interview. You can and should, of course, discuss interviewees' performance of the duties of their offices or jobs – what they are being paid for – but it is easier to do that if both of you know that some progressive objectives covering all or parts of the job will be under review. Somehow people are less inclined to take on board suggestions or criticisms which come 'out of the blue' and relate to a general function of their job, such as being nice to customers. In fact the giving and receiving of criticism is one of the most difficult chapters in the art of communication. Remember Adam and Eve?

> *Thus they in mutual accusation spent*
> *The fruitless hours, neither self-condemning*

Milton's evocation of their expulsion from the Garden of Eden in *Paradise Lost* may sound echoes in an experienced manager's mind. It is all too easy for an appraisal interview, in which one person attempts to point out to another his or her shortcomings and failings, to develop into a Miltonian slanging match of attack and counter-attack, accusation and defence. Moreover, much more emphasis is now being placed on the formal appraisal interview designed to assess work performance at regular intervals. Too often the 'how to do it' handbooks on appraisal interviews only stress the formal aspects: the value of organizing and regularizing what is in fact a natural feature of good leadership. They ignore the major problems of communications in such situations; they overlook the common experience that the giving and receiving of praise or criticism come highest on the list of difficult conversations.

Here I propose to concentrate on the exchange of praise and criticism, those precious but unstable commodities which can make or break individuals, teams and even organizations. Moreover, it would be a mistake to limit the consideration of them entirely to the formal appraisal interview: we may find ourselves dealing in praise or criticism – on the sending or receiving end – at any time of the day or night and at any place, be it the boardroom or the washroom or at home!

Just as a good reader makes a good book, so a good interviewee or listener makes for an effective appraisal. As the writer of the biblical *Book of Proverbs* noted: 'He who corrects a scoffer gets himself abuse, and he who reproves a wicked man incurs injury. Do not reprove a scoffer, or he will hate you; reprove a wise man and he will love you. Give instruction to a wise man and he will be still wiser. A good receiver is essential if there is to be any genuine praise or constructive criticism at all.'

The word *praise* or *appraisal* comes from a Latin verb meaning to set a price or value on something. Thus in one of the first printed books Thomas Caxton could write: 'They preysed nothing the thinges that were erthely.' Our verb *to prize* approximates it. *Evaluationg* means virtually the same as appraising. Elsewhere I have suggested that valuing (along with analysing and synthesizing) is one of the fundamental movements of our minds: we cannot avoid doing it without an effort, and then only for very short times. Thus appraisal or evaluation lies on the trade routes of our minds quite naturally.

Praise implies a positive evaluation of worth, excellence or merit which is communicated.

In order to have value it must be given sparingly. For praise, like gold and diamonds, owes its value only to its scarcity.

Like praise, *criticism* was originally a neutral word, and this meaning survives in the phrase 'literary criticism'. Stemming from the Greek word for a judge, it has arrived at a sense of a 'guilty' verdict, a negative evaluation. Most people are aware, however, of the distinction between *constructive* and *negative* criticism, the former being positive in tone and accompanied by practical suggestions for improvement.

Most praise and criticism is rightly directed towards performance, or what a person *does* rather than what he or she *is*. On the other hand the distinction between doing and being is a fluid one: to some extent our actions are fruits of our character, and our character is the by-product of our actions. 'The bird carries the wings, and the wings support the bird', as the proverb says. It is fatally easy, however, to draw false conclusions about character from observations of a person's work.

As a general rule, for that reason, it is often suggested that appraisal conversations should stop short at comments about performance, and eschew any reactions to character. But there are obvious exceptions to such a commonsense rule. We all need a certain balance of self-esteem. That balance is always shifting. Sometimes we respect our own conduct or stance; sometimes we feel guilty and despise ourselves; sometimes we fall into bouts of self-pity. In the hours when our proper level of self-confidence is slipping, a good leader or friend may deftly and tactfully restore our sense of self-value by some more realistic and encouraging evaluation of our character. At other moments, when self-esteem is threatening to collapse into the rubble of conceit and vanity, those afflictions which eventually impair judgement and weaken relationships, a quiet word from someone who cares can restore a more balanced sense of our worth.

Because of the connecting passage between doing and being it is important to shut the door between them as firmly as possible, so that you can comment on performance without the person concerned feeling that their whole life and personality are under scrutiny. Moreover, like a medieval confessor, you should not offer appraisal unless you are willing to undergo appraisal yourself. And you should offer your comments in such a way that you maintain, restore, or enhance the other person's sense of value, which is one of our most precious possessions.

People on the receiving end of praise often exhibit what seems to be embarrassment, as if they do not know how to respond. Some social psychologists have interpreted these reactions as evidence that people sense the potential use of praise to manipulate them. Certainly the unease may be a sign that the person being praised sees through the false motives or insincerity behind the compliments. On the other hand it may be modesty at work.

Modesty is the active way that a good person responds to praise from others. In Latin *modus* means a measure. A modest person checks the praise given against their own measure. If the praiser has made a mistake, and given too much credit, he or she will politely return it to the sender by pointing out the facts. For example, they might draw attention to the contribution of other people to the meritorious actions or performance. Moreover, the praiser and the praised may be operating on different measures. Thus it is a natural instinct for modest people, who have enough self-esteem already, to deflect praise to the earth like lightning, so that it does not go to their heads. And the most effective way of doing this is to share it with others.

To reject praise absolutely, however, can be an immodest act. More accurately, it is false modesty. It denies the value or truth of someone else's statement, making them into a liar or a fraud. It denies the inherent social nature of our lives: that living consists of receiving gracefully as well as giving generously. It dries up one of the natural sources of strength and gratitude in society. Above all it is phoney or unreal.

GIVING CONSTRUCTIVE CRITICISM

If it is not always easy to receive praise gracefully in the spirit in which it was intended, by common consent, it is much harder to accept criticism. Therefore it is much more difficult to criticize others well. Through experience most of us learn some commonsense rules for both giving and receiving criticism, for work judged to be below the accepted or necessary standard of performance. For example, as already mentioned, most of us appreciate criticism which is followed by *constructive* suggestions on how to improve up to and beyond the required minimum standard.

We tend to assume that criticism flows downwards, as it did when we were children. But in organizations criticism flows inwards (in the form of customer complaints), upwards and sideways. The increasing use of '360° appraisal' – assessment by colleagues and subordinates as well as superiors – is one organizational form of that social reality.

Whether inwards, downwards, upwards or sideways, criticism often takes the form of *complaint*. Complaining is the act of finding fault with your circumstances or treatment. It may be a justified or unjustified dissatisfaction. When you complain you are expressing in words your grief, pain or discontent. It may lead on to a formal accusation or charge.

Most complaints about someone's work imply a gap between expectation and performance. Where the complainer is ignorant of how the gap can be bridged a mere complaint is all that can be expected from him or her. For example, you may complain to the doctor if the medicine prescribed actually makes you worse; you can hardly nominate an alternative. In appraising the work of those who report to you, however, you ought to be able to offer constructive criticism, i.e. some suggestions on how the work can be improved. If you cannot do that it is doubtful whether or not you have the right to lead or manage.

Here are some ground rules for easing difficult conversations. With experience you may modify, or even occasionally omit, one or more of them – providing you know what you are doing. Can you add to the list?

Offer criticisms in private if possible, and do not spread them unnecessarily

Any effective criticism may sting a little. Your indifference to your colleague's feelings, displayed by a willingness to criticize in front of others, will be taken at least as seriously as the content of what you say. In fairness to him or her, and yourself, wait until you are alone.

Avoid long or predictable preambles

Avoid prefaces such as 'Listen. There's something I've wanted to tell you for a long time. It may hurt you, but . . .' In these matters it is best to come to the point without beating the daylights out of the proverbial bush. Nor should criticisms be invariably prefaced by positive evaluations which contain very little supplementary information, such as 'You are doing a fine job, but . . .' Don't use insincere praise as a sweetener. 'He who praises everybody praises nobody,' wrote Samuel Johnson. But of course criticism will always be more readily received if you can preface it with some genuine and evidence-based praise.

Keep it as simple and as accurate as possible

Avoid overload. Try to make only one or two major criticisms at a time, rather than presenting a list of sixty or seventy! Criticisms should not be allowed to pile up. Too many major and minor points thrown together reduce clarity and are ineffective, because no one can handle that amount of critical comment. As the Chinese proverb says: 'Do not use a hatchet to remove a fly from your friend's forehead.' Nor should the simple point be endlessly repeated. The reward for good listening ought to be exemption from hearing the same shortcoming discussed again.

Exaggerations intended for emphasis, signalled by such words as *always* and *never*, rob you of your accuracy and the psychological advantages that go with it. Moreover, instead of statements such as 'You are very idle' it may be usually more accurate to say, 'You give me the impression of being lazy.' For that impression at least is an objective fact. And if more than one person has formed that impression it should have some weight (see page 45).

Offer only constructive criticism of actions that can be changed

'No man, by taking thought, can add one cubit to his stature,' said Jesus. It is useless to criticize people for characteristics which they cannot change. Such personal remarks should be avoided. Whether or not characteristics fall into this category is a matter of judgement. After all, someone once defined character as what you have done with your personality.

Don't compare the person's behaviour with that of others

Comparisons are especially odious in appraisal conversations. No one wants to be described as inferior. Comparisons predispose others not to listen, even when the criticism or complaint is justified.

Don't talk about other people's motives when making a complaint or criticism

Motives stand closer to the inner person than his or her actions, and to pass judgement on them can be interpreted as a censure of the whole person.

Moreover, actions are often multi-motivated, and it is fatally easy for an observer to draw the wrong conclusions about these hidden springs of behaviour, especially when the interviewee is only dimly aware of why he or she does or does not do certain things. Don't confuse consequence and intention.

Always be able to back up your observations with some evidence or data. Thus an appraisal should never stray far from the facts. Avoid amateur psychology.

After making a criticism in good faith, don't apologize for it

Apology may fuel some inner doubt as to whether or not you had the right to say what you did. It is asking the other person to brace you against the stress of criticizing him or her. It imposes an unnecessary burden on them. An apologetic tone and embarrassed manner does neither of you any good. You do need moral courage. But by all means apologize if it transpires that you have got the facts wrong. It is more fitting to thank the person concerned for listening to your criticism or complaint.

In summary, giving constructive criticism is never going to be easy. If you can avoid having to do so that is an advantage. One useful strategy is to encourage interviewees to appraise themselves. For where possible, people should be encouraged to be self-critical — critical of their own performance and motivated to improve. This approach goes a long way to remove the unnecessary conflict from the meeting. Your role then becomes one of modifying, supplementing or pointing up that self-criticism as a prelude to action.

'No man can tell another his faults so as to benefit him, unless he loves him,' said Henry Ward Beecher. Love, in the sense of taking the other person's interests seriously, stands here at the core of good communication.

ON THE RECEIVING END

'A blind man will not thank you for a looking-glass,' says an eighteenth-century English proverb. Assuming you are not blind in the inward eyes, however, you should work with your critic to identify the area for improvement, like a fellow surgeon working around an operating table. What should matter to both of you is any improvement in your common work. Nor will you be distracted by imperfections in your appointed (or self-appointed) critic: truth is truth whether it comes from the mouths of angels or barmaids. Try to be grateful in advance for what you are about to receive.

Be quiet while you are being criticized, and make it clear that you are listening
Whether you agree or not is an issue to be discussed later. Look directly at the person talking to you. Only thus can you convey that you are open to what he or she is saying. Gazing out of the window is not so convincing!

Under no condition find fault with the person who has just criticized you
If he or she has used the wrong words, for example, or got a minor fact wrong, do not overreact, wait half an hour. If you counter-attack by reciprocating the criticism – 'Now I think about it, you come late to meetings too' – this implies that you interpret it as an insult. Or you become so busy in marshalling your own forces for the attack that you neglect to heed what is actually being said.

Don't create the impression that the other person is destroying your spirit
Some people can be belligerent at first, and then start acting as though they were at the edge of despair. Don't try to manipulate the appraiser by appearing completely defeated.

Don't try to change the subject
Humour is a way of keeping matters in proportion, but a flippant reaction suggests that a person cannot take criticism seriously. Changing the subject is a more extreme form of taking flight from the issue. Use your mind to help articulate the objection, not to make it disappear.

Don't caricature the complaint

If a person says you were *thoughtless*, don't ascribe to them the statement that you are irresponsible and then defend yourself against a charge that has not been made. The deliberate exaggeration of a charge against you is a tactic for avoiding it.

Don't assume that your critic has some ulterior, hostile motive

Take the criticism at face value. The question about the interviewer's motives should come later, if at all.

Convey to the other person that you understand his objection

Paraphrasing or using a minor question is one good way of doing this. In effect you are saying that the message is received and noted.

Don't let people get at you on the pretext that they are giving you constructive criticism. You have the right at any time, I believe, to turn off the tap of criticism. Refusal to allow you to do so suggests a compulsive critic at work. If you are out to beat a dog you're sure to find a stick. The path is narrow: you must be open to criticism but subject it to examination before accepting it.

To receive criticism well and to act upon it is the ultimate badge of the good listener. If it is unjustified, as later certified by completely impartial 'appeal judges', the appraisal interview can still be creatively turned into an occasion for learning humility.

If you feel that the criticism is fully justified, or at least that there is something in it for further reflection, thank your critics for their time and effort. 'Take each man's censure, but reserve your judgement,' as Shakespeare puts it in *Hamlet*. They have done you a personal favour; they have given you a present. 'Criticism is a study by which people grow more important and formidable at very small expense,' concluded Samuel Johnson. Can you afford to ignore such valuable and free tuition?

HOW DO YOU HANDLE CRITICISM?

An advice columnist once wrote that 'The best way to measure people is to watch the way they behave when you offer them something for free.'

I think you can tell even more about people by how they react when you offer them criticism.

People generally respond to criticism, constructive or otherwise, in four stages.

1. *They ignore it*
This is the response of dullards and incompetents. They have no idea what you're talking about, why you're telling them, or what they can do about it. They have no business being in your company.

2. *They deny it*
This is often a sign of a dangerously selective mind. You have to wonder what else this person is leaving out in his dealings outside the company and in his communications within.

3. *They deflect it*
This is the response of the master politician. When he's on the spot, he always seems to know more about what everyone else is (or is not) doing than he knows about himself. Quite often, he doesn't even realize he's blaming others for his failings. That makes it vital that you do.

> *4. They accept it*
> This is a sign of emotional maturity. The people who can accept responsibility for a problem – whether they're directly at fault or not – are generally the only people who can correct it.
>
> The people I admire – and prefer to hire – progress the first three stages very quickly.
>
> Mark McCormack, Business Age, July 1992

THE TOUCHSTONE OF EFFECTIVENESS

You may wish to remind yourself at this point of the distinction between *response* and *effect*, and the model on page 29. Sometimes there will be an immediate negative reaction against a justified criticism, even a rejection of it. Later, however, an observer might see that the person concerned is actually working in a different and improved way. Consciously the criticism and the 'critic' have been rejected; unconsciously, or in the depth mind, the message has been hoisted in, and transformed into action. In such instances the appraiser will receive no credit, no reward of gratitude from the other person. But leadership does not entitle one to such rewards. Anyway, the proportion of those people who are likely to return thanks for such personal help is probably no more than about one in ten.

It may be useful to the appraiser to recall that he or she is addressing a person's subconscious or depth mind through the gateways of the senses. And it sometimes takes time for the penny to drop, as we say. A second or third interview or conversation may become necessary, for repetition on different occasions, couched in other words and images, may implant a message more firmly. Yet the balance is fine. We have to guard always 'the sacred right of rejection'. If the message is repeatedly rejected then the appraiser has to reconsider his advice. It may be possible to accept the differences of opinion bravely. On the other hand, the interviewee's prospects or even very employment may rest upon their acceptance of the proposed improvement. If this is so, it is of course essential that it is made absolutely clear during the interview or course of interviews, with some deadlines also clearly set out.

The good leader uses his power of praising or criticizing judiciously to achieve good purposes, while building up the community and forwarding the growth of individuals. With regard to the latter, he might well meditate occasionally on the prayer of the Psalmist: 'Let the righteous rather smite me friendly: and reprove me. But let not their precious balms break my head.'

This consideration of the difficulties of giving and receiving of both praise the criticism leads us back to the centrality for good communication of integrity, both in its professional and personal senses. Integrity is the quality which makes people trust one another. It is the bedrock on which a lasting relationship can be built, one which can take the exchange of meanings, however unpalatable, because the end is to edify or build you up. As Peter Drucker said in *The Practice of Management* (1956):

When all is said and done, developing men still requires a basic quality in the manager which cannot be created by supplying skills or by emphasizing the importance of the task. It requires integrity of character . . . It may be argued that every occupation – the doctor, the lawyer, the grocer – requires integrity. But there is a difference. The manager lives with the people he manages, he decides what their work is to be, he directs it, he trains them for it, he appraises it and, often, he decides their future. The relationship of merchant and client requires honourable dealings. Being a manager, though, is more like being a parent, or a teacher. And in these relationships honourable dealings are not enough; personal integrity is of the essence.

KEY POINTS

- Interviews or personal meetings – usually between two people – are an integral part of professional life. They can be classified according to their purpose, but they share in common certain characteristics: they are usually prearranged, require preparation and a definite purpose, and the people involved participate in well-defined roles.
- The principles of clarity, preparation, simplicity, naturalness and conciseness should inform or govern the exchange of information and meaning that lies at the core of an interview. Together, they spell effectiveness.
- As an interviewer you are in the lead role. You have to take charge in a pleasant but firm way, and guide the discussion to a clear and successful conclusion, if possible for both parties.
- There are few techniques in interviewing that really matter, beyond the ability to keep your mouth shut for as much of the time as possible. But you should develop the skill of both knowing the range of possible questions and choosing the right one at the right time, like a carpenter selecting just the best chisel for a particular job.
- Giving praise and criticism in relation to performance isn't easy, which is why many appraisal interviews are such unsatisfactory affairs. By applying and practising the

ground rules listed in this chapter you can make a significant improvement in your effectiveness as an appraiser.

- But can you take criticism yourself? Again this chapter has listed some commonsense guidelines for getting the best out of being appraised. Look upon your next performance appraisal as not a threat but an opportunity.

The deepest principle in human nature is the craving to be appreciated.

William James

9

LEADING EFFECTIVE MEETINGS

'Nothing is impossible until it is sent to a committee,' said one manager in a large organization somewhat despairingly at a recent conference on innovation. Meetings proliferate, but they have acquired a bad name for ineffectiveness, time wasting and sheer lack of fun.

> *When shall we three meet again*
> *In thunder, lightning, or in rain?*

Managers will certainly meet in better conditions than those witches in Shakespeare's *Macbeth* on their blasted heath, but they definitely know that they will be meeting again — and again!

Meeting is a very general word which encompasses any situation in which two or more people come together by accident or design, in an encounter which may be momentary or prolonged. Almost all of them involve some form of communication. But the meetings which concern us in this chapter are those which involve a group of people met for discussion. How do you lead or manage that discussion effectively?

THE ROLE OF DISCUSSION

Discussion suggests to some a rambling or free-wheeling conversation in which people express their views or sentiments to each other – just the sort of thing to be banned from efficient, tightly controlled and brisk meetings! But, rightly understood, discussion lies at the core of all purposeful meetings. It should be differentiated from conversation on the one hand, and a formal debate on the other. It ought to be limited to a given theme. More often than not, discussion is a way of reaching conclusions or determining a course of action.

The actual word *discussion* comes from a Latin root that means 'to shake apart'. Possibilities are sifted or shaken apart. Their pros and cons are considered. For this work to be done effectively, five ingredients need to be present:

- *Planning* in advance is essential to successful discussion. It is futile to rely upon spontaneous combustion to develop profitable talk. The initiative for this planning may be taken by a designated leader, but it is better when at least some members of the group can work on it together.
- *Informality* is desirable to encourage the fullest possible participation, although the size of the group or audience and the seating arrangements in the meeting place impose some limits. Organized informality best describes this objective.
- *Participation* is an essential ingredient of good discussion, for this method assumes that each individual may have something of value to contribute, and that the co-operative pooling of all available information is the best way to find the right solution. In small groups everyone who wishes to may speak; in a large public discussion only a few can get

the floor, but it should be emphasized that active listening is participation.

- *Purpose* is essential in good discussion. Merely pleasant or socially useful talk that skips from one topic to another is not discussion as conceived here.
- *Leadership*, in some form, is necessary for a successful discussion. In public meetings the leader or chairman may be assisted by a secretary. In small groups whose members know each other, the functions of leadership may sometimes be shared by various individuals.

THE SEATING PLAN

The leader's responsibility for planning starts before the meeting in question begins. By using common sense, laced with some visual imagination, he or she should be able to foresee what will be required in or near the place of meeting. In particular they ought to look at the seating arrangements, because sometimes these can impose their own (often unwelcome) pattern on the exchange of information and ideas, as one of King James I's chief ministers, Francis Bacon, observed over three hundred years ago:

A long table and a square table, or seats about the walls, seem things of form, but are things of substance; for at a long table a few at the upper end, in effect, sway all the business; but in the other form there is more use of the counsellors' opinions that sit lower. A king, when he presides in council, let him beware how he opens his own inclination too much in that which he propounds; for else counsellors will but take the wind of him, and, instead of giving free counsel, will sing him a song of 'I shall please'.

The varieties of discussion, private and public, are endless. But, as a rule, the general purpose of the meeting, the size of the group, and its progress in analysing the problem, should determine the form of discussion used in a particular situation. A *committee*, for example, is a small group, appointed by the parent organization, which meets to investigate a problem and, later, to formulate its report and recommendation. At a *conference*, by contrast, delegates representing various organizations, sometimes co-operative, sometimes hostile, meet to consider a problem and, if possible, to recommend a joint course of action. At other times a conference (alias workshop or seminar) may have as its only purpose the acquiring of new knowledge or skills by those taking part.

The terms *leader* and *chairman* are used almost inter-changeably by writers on meetings. There is a tendency, however, to speak of *leaders* of informal group discussion and *chairman* of committees, conferences or public meetings – the more formal occasions. *Chair* or *chairperson* is now sometimes substituted for the latter in the interests of 'political correctness', but most people are still happy with *chairman*, for *man* is a synonym for humanity as well as the name of one of its two constituent sexes.

If you are a manager, it follows, you will probably have to chair meetings in the formal sense and also lead discussion. These roles are occasionally separated but more often they go hand in hand. It is not always easy to combine them, for it is like being both a football referee and the captain of a side at the same time.

BE CLEAR ABOUT PURPOSE

Discussion can serve a variety of purposes. Even within a single meeting it may change gear from one to another. Here are some of these general purposes:

- to exchange information
- to make decisions
- to release tensions
- to form attitudes
- to instruct or teach

These purposes are not mutually exclusive. Pooling available information, for example, often precedes and accompanies decision making. It may relieve tension! Again, as another example, early research in this field suggests that those who gain the most information through discussion are most likely to change their attitudes.

BE PREPARED BEFORE THE MEETING

The general purpose of the meeting needs to be broken down into more tangible aims – directional but open-ended – and more specific objectives or targets. Once more the principle of Be Prepared comes into play as you begin to think ahead and plan the meeting in more detail. For careful preparation is the secret of success.

The agenda is a key factor. It shouldn't be just a list of headings to jog your memory during a meeting. Draw it up with thought, indicating whether an item is for discussion or decision. Briefly describe the matter or subject.

'Mounting costs', for example, looks too brief and vague, whereas 'Mounting costs: to discuss the report on energy conservation in the factory and make decisions on the first and third recommendations on p. 16' is much more definite. It gives people the opportunity to think about the matter beforehand. Ensure that everyone receives the agenda and relevant papers – in this case the energy conservation report – at least five clear days before the meeting.

People take in information more readily through their eyes than their ears – hence the Chinese proverb quoted in Chapter 7, 'A picture is worth a thousand words'. Visual aids should therefore play a part in your meetings more often than not: if they are clear, simple and vivid they can save you time.

Exercise: Be Prepared

Identify the next three formal meetings which you will chair. Jot them down on a piece of paper and label them A, B and C. Do you intend to make use of any of the following:

	A	B	C
• Overhead projector	...	...	...
• Slides	...	...	...
• Prepared flipcharts	...	...	...
• Unprepared flipcharting	...	...	...
• Reports	...	...	...
• Financial statements	...	...	...
• A written agenda	...	...	...
• Models	...	...	...
• Minutes	...	...	...
• A different room layout	...	...	...

Time spent on preparation is seldom wasted. If you go into a meeting clear about the objectives, having thought about the subject in advance and with everything ready, it is already most probable that your meeting will be effective.

CHECKLIST: PREPARING FOR DISCUSSION

	Yes	No
Are you clear about the purpose of this planned discussion?	❑	❑
Do the other participants know that purpose?	❑	❑
If not, do you plan to communicate it to them before the meeting?	❑	❑
Have you circulated any necessary information well before the meeting?	❑	❑
Have you identified the main topics to be discussed? Is each objective clear?	❑	❑
Have you framed some questions to stimulate discussion?	❑	❑
Have you prepared a timetable for the meeting?	❑	❑
Is the accommodation and seating plan arranged?	❑	❑
Are all necessary materials, including visual aids and flipcharts, ready?	❑	❑

GUIDING THE DISCUSSION

As a chairman yourself it is useful to bear in mind that you have two principal functions within your role. Being chairman in the narrow sense means you are accountable for seeing that procedures are adhered to and that participants both behave themselves and contribute as effectively as possible to the business in hand. You are there to see fair play, to ensure that everyone has their turn and to apply the appropriate rules, not unlike a referee. The foreman of a jury is a chairman in this specific sense.

Second, you may be the group's leader or manager as well, charged with achieving specified results. The nature of those outcomes will necessarily vary according to the type of meeting (see Figure 9.1). In creative-thinking meetings, for example, the leader's role may be more that of a catalyst than traffic controller.

There can be some obvious tensions between the 'referee' and 'leader' roles. Some groups and leaders indeed seek to avoid them by appointing a referee-type chairman, like the Speaker in the House of Commons, leaving leaders free to argue their case in the meeting without having to preside over it. Other chairmen signal when they are changing hats by 'stepping down from the chair' for a particular item on the agenda.

In most situations it makes sense for the chairman to exercise both functions. There is some overlap between the roles anyway. Let us assume here that you are doing both.

Some of the key leadership functions, such as *defining the task* and *planning*, have been discussed above. But as chairman you should remember to begin the meeting by saying what the purpose is and why it is necessary. Don't assume that everyone knows. You may also want to check that the participants are comfortable with the agenda, so that *your* plan for the meeting now becomes *our* plan for it. In a pleasant but firm way, show that you have taken charge.

Once work has started on the agenda you will have to exercise the function of *controlling*, which should be done with intelligence and sensitivity. What would you do about an over-talkative person? It is essential to stop him but it has to be done tactfully as well as firmly: 'Thank you, Michael, I think we have got the drift of your argument. Susan, you haven't said anything yet. Do you agree with Michael or not?'

Experienced colleagues at a discussion meeting will seldom require you to exercise this *gate-keeping* function of 'opening the door' for someone to make a contribution beyond listening intently. More often than not, your energies will be deployed in shutting the door! But as a leader you should always be aware of who hasn't contributed, and if you think that diffidence or lack of assertiveness to jump into the busy pool is the reason, you can at least offer an opportunity for speaking.

If a long-winded person still challenges you for the right of way – by continuing to talk over others or by interrupting again – then you will have to show more steel until the message is taken. Never lose control.

Heading off potential or actual irrelevancies is also a vital part of controlling a meeting. Sometimes a red herring looks more tasty than the bread-and-butter items on the agenda. Where the object of a meeting is creative thinking, as in brainstorming sessions, it is often worth pursuing red herrings, for the apparently irrelevant may disguise the germ of a new idea.

The problems of controlling or guiding a discussion are

heightened by the fact that it is in the nature of the beast to ramble and become discursive. As the model below suggests, the complex pattern of lines of communication available in a group situation (as opposed to a one-to-one interview) makes control that much more difficult. Some formal groups, in the parliamentary tradition, try to solve that potential difficulty by making it a rule that all remarks should be made to and through the chairman. That may work in more formal debate, especially if it involves a large number of people, but it is antithetical to the more informal and group-centred nature of discussion.

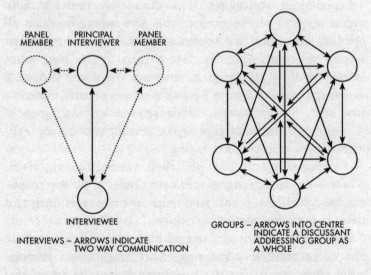

Figure 9.1 *Lines of communication*

To exercise these leadership functions and to contribute to the discussion, you will need to develop yourself by becoming:

- a clear and rapid thinker
- an attentive listener
- able to express yourself clearly and succinctly
- ready to clarify views badly expressed
- able to be impartial and impersonal
- a preventer of inappropriate interruptions
- patient, tolerant and kind
- friendly but brisk and businesslike

One important way of guiding the discussion is to *summarize* progress so far, so that the remaining agenda or issues stand out clearly. Thus a summary given during a meeting (rather than in conclusion) can act as a trumpet sounding the recall. But the summary has to be accurate. With all their other responsibilities it requires a high level of natural ability and practice for leaders to be able to summarize succinctly at the right time, in such a way that the summary is instantly accepted as a true account of the proceedings to date.

Although *summarizing* is an especially important skill for a chairman, all listeners can find it useful on occasions. A summary is a sign of listening because it establishes whether or not you can select the salient points to the satisfaction of the speaker and the rest of the audience, if there is one. A summary not only chops away much of the dead wood and foliage, but it also provides a listening check, for other listeners will either accept your abbreviation or reject it. Thus a summary helps the process of thought and digestion.

The singer, however, takes a piano note and transforms it into a vocal sound. Another chairmanship asset is the distinctively human ability to *interpret* from one language into another, without loss of fidelity to the original. The interpreter must be able to divine meaning and translate it into a different language. For example, the contribution of a technical specialist may have to be translated into language simple enough to be understood with reasonable effort around the table. Your ability to do so will test your powers as a listener. But such a timely interpretation can contribute to the overall direction of the discussion.

Your manner may do as much if not more than your words to encourage (or discourage) genuine communication. Humour, modesty and firmness have their own part to play. As the leader's own task encompasses the creation of a warm, friendly but businesslike atmosphere, it is vital that you should check whether or not your manner aids and abets in promoting good communication. In the right time and place, ask for feedback on this score. Remember the cautionary case study of Alistair Jackson (see pages 42–4).

If someone is asked to take action as a result of discussion on an item, the chairman should check that the participant understands and accepts that action. Steps or actions thus agreed should normally carry a completion time.

The questions as to whether a committee – a decision-making or problem-solving group – can be executive, i.e. can do anything on its own – is really trivial. Literally as a body it can no more do anything than a football team can score a goal. In each case there must be an individual agent, but it is the group which makes it possible for the individual to act. Although its decision will in most cases be carried out by one of its members, or its officers, in a real sense the action is the action of the committee. The important decision has been made by the committee, or is a consequence of its deliberations.

THE EFFECTIVE CHAIRMAN

The Prime Minister shouldn't speak too much himself in Cabinet. He should start the show or ask somebody else to do so, and then intervene only to bring out the more modest chaps who, despite their seniority, might say nothing if not asked. And the Prime Minister must sum up . . . Particularly when a non-Cabinet minister is asked to attend, especially if it is his first time, the Prime Minister may have to be cruel. The visitor may want to show how good he is, and go on too long. A good thing is to take no chance and ask him to send the Cabinet a paper in advance . . . If somebody else looks like making a speech, it is sound to nip in with, 'Are you *objecting*? You're not? Right. Next business', and the Cabinet can move on leaving in its wake a trail of clear, crisp uncompromising decisions. That is what government is about. And the challenge to democracy is to get it done quickly.

Clement Attlee

Remember that discussion is a slow process. It's inappropriate when quick action is required. Nor has it much value in problem solving if group members lack relevant knowledge or information. Moreover, the informality inherent in discussion means that it is no substitute for a comprehensive statement of all the issues or a sustained presentation of an argument. Lastly, the prospect of discussion seldom encourages thorough or meticulous preparation compared to, say, if you were asked to give a presentation. The results may be poor-quality thinking and inadequate decisions.

These limitations of discussion should not be made into an excuse to dispense with it or to cut it down to the bare minimum. Leadership can hardly be democratic if there is no discussion. They only emphasize the necessity for its *intelligent* use, on the right kinds of topics and problems, after adequate planning, and under optimum conditions of leadership and teamwork.

Aim	START ON TIME
	OUTLINE PURPOSE CLEARLY
	State problem/situation/reason
	Define constraints and limitations
	Establish task(s) of meetings
Plan	PREPARE THE AGENDA
	Draw up the agenda
	Make sure that items on it are prioritized and allocated sufficient time
Guide	ENSURE EFFECTIVE DISCUSSION
	Introduce topic(s) for discussion
	Draw out opinions, viewpoints and experiences
	Develop group interest and involvement
	Keep discussion within stated task(s)
	Use time constraints to maintain relevance
Crystallize	ESTABLISH CONCLUSIONS
	Recognize degrees of feeling and changes of opinion
	Summarize points of agreement and disagreement
	State intermediate conclusions as they are reached
	Check understanding and acceptance

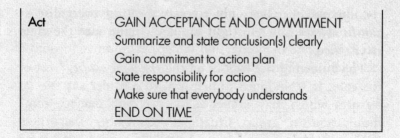

Act	GAIN ACCEPTANCE AND COMMITMENT
	Summarize and state conclusion(s) clearly
	Gain commitment to action plan
	State responsibility for action
	Make sure that everybody understands
	END ON TIME

Figure 9.2 *Making meetings effective*

Good chairmanship is vital for effective meetings. The chairman's task will sometimes pose problems, but a good chairman can make sure that a meeting is punctual, covers the ground, keeps moving forward and makes the appropriate decisions. Beneath that process lies purposeful communication.

UNDERSTANDING GROUPS

There are forces or factors in all groups which can affect the free exchange of information and meaning for better or worse. As a leader of discussion you need to be aware of them.

All working groups have three areas of need in common: the need to achieve their common task, the need to maintain themselves as a working unity, and the needs of individual members. Although it is composed of individuals, a group soon develops a 'group personality'.

As a leader you should always balance what groups have in common with what makes them unique and irreplaceable. The former allows you to prepare for your role, knowing what functions will be required. The latter reminds you that every group, every meeting, every discussion is always different. You can never jump into the same river twice.

The following list focuses on the *group personality* facet of the coin. It is designed to help you to consider any special features which may influence the way you manage communication in group situations. Remember that these factors develop only after a group has been together for some time.

- *Group conformity*   Most of us tend to behave in ways that will gain recognition, admiration, respect or approval from the groups to which we belong. Through trial and error we have learnt that if we conform to accepted standards our group relationships are happier. Thus our beliefs and actions are often influenced more by group opinion than by expert opinion. This is not a rule without exceptions, but it is common enough to be a significant characteristic of group personality. The degree of conformity determines how free members feel to express their own ideas, and how much these ideas are appreciated by others.

- *Group values*   Any group is likely to endorse and maintain values, or ideals, which differentiate it from others. An analysis of these values will aid in understanding a group's personality. It may also explain the aggressiveness one group displays towards others. And such an analysis of group values will provide a basis for predicting the programmes, activities and actions a group is likely to support.

- *Group attitude to change*   Social changes within or among groups seldom win complete and immediate acceptance. Thus the degree to which a group resists change, either within the group or in its relations with others, is an important index of the group personality. Equally characteristic may be the group's standard methods for effecting change, whether by dictation of the leader, consensus, or some 'middle way'.

- *Group prejudice* Few of us willingly admit to holding prejudices which make us intolerant of other people's sex, race, religion, nationality, or social status. But we do know that other people are often prejudiced! In groups of like-minded people prejudice is often clearly evident. In fact the prejudice of individuals may be intensified when they are within their group, and apparent even when they are apart from their fellows.

- *Group power* Groups as wholes are always stronger than the sum of their individual parts. The social force of feeling and opinion is so powerful that people can fall sick and die if they are ostracized by their fellows. Indeed, in primitive societies to turn your face away from someone is a severe punishment. For we need people who will 'countenance' us, or turn a friendly face towards us. In groups we remain aware of these primeval forces in our depth minds: hence the shades of our reactive feelings, which range from shyness through to a proper respect for the power of the community. For this reason individuals may find it difficult to speak their minds in groups. The leader, who has a certain counter-balancing power *vis-à-vis* the group, can support the individual in a variety of ways, but first you need to sense the balance of power between the group as a whole and each individual.

All the characteristics of group personality listed above will influence the method and effectiveness of group discussion. Suppose, for example, that a group has a high regard for majority rule, is accustomed to formal meetings and enforces strict parliamentary rules, makes little resistance to change, encourages members with differing opinions to speak freely and has few strong prejudices. For such a group, one might be able to predict with considerable accuracy the patterns of discussion most likely to be followed, and to estimate their probable effectiveness.

You also need to know how decisions are taken. In some groups decisions are made by one individual. In more democratic groups decisions are made by *enumeration*, counting votes after adequate discussion. In others, decisions represent a *compromise* between proponents and opponents of a course of action in which members yield part of their views to reach a decision. In a very real sense, a democracy is government by compromise. Under the most favourable conditions, groups may reach decisions by *consensus*, a synthesis of the views of all group members. These favourable conditions seldom exist if a group feels outside pressure, works under a state of tension or to meet a deadline.

An important skill in this context is *testing for commitment*. Not all decisions should be made by consensus, or even by majority vote, but in a democratic society many should be. Moreover, the closer a group comes to consensus the more its members will tend to feel involved, committed or responsible for the outcome. Consensus, incidentally, does not mean total 100 per cent agreement on the part of each individual. Rather, consensus stands for the decision which everyone will accept and go along with as the best in the circumstances. In physiology it means the general accord of different organs of the body in effecting a given purpose.

Some leaders possess a natural awareness of the consentive feeling in a group; others develop it over a lifetime. Of course, knowing where the consensus lies does not necessarily mean that the leader accepts the group direction. He may seek to change, or influence it, or – in the last resort – tender his resignation. But whatever his ultimate response, it is a good start for him if he can sense the invisible consensus. Groups, like moving shoals of fish, have an unseen centre point; a constantly shifting pole which draws the fish together as if by magnetic influence. Consensus in human groups is a similar centre of feelings. No leader can afford to be so oblivious to this point or so far ahead of it that all contact is lost.

Thus, like Moses, the leader has to know when and where to strike the water of consensus from the rock of outward appearance. It is not always evident where the water lies, and the leader of any meeting should be able to test for consensus. Like water-divining, this is an inexact science. It is made up of simultaneously asking for people's views while watching their faces and expressions. Views may be elicited either by direct questions, or else putting forward a trial consensus and judging the reactions. In this case testing for consensus is akin to summary.

What has to be avoided is making mistaken assumptions about group consensus, based on a misinterpretation of one or two nods or smiles, a few murmurs of approval or the outpourings of a voluble self-appointed spokesman. When leaders seize upon such straws, they either reveal their incompetence or (even worse) their own wishful thinking about the result. Worst of all, it may look as if they are seeking to impose their own will by underhand methods.

The process of finding consensus is fraught with hazards, especially if some sort of consentive action is desperately needed. In particular the leader may have to guard against unfair pressures being brought to bear on individuals. 'We do *all* agree, don't we, Michael . . .?' As the clock warns that the end of the meeting is nigh, it is common for waves of hostile or angry feelings, separated by troughs of honeyed smiles, to wash against the opposition in a last attempt to wear it away. Like the false prophets, such groups show themselves anxious 'to cry peace, peace, where there is no peace'.

In the absence of consensus groups usually have alternative systems for making up their minds. The most common of these is *voting*. Depending on the rules, a vote may be carried either by a simple majority, even if it is only one, or else a predetermined proportion, e.g. two-thirds, or even 75 per cent. This method is said to have the disadvantage that it leaves an unconvinced minority. But this is mitigated where the minority, having had their say, are willing to go along with the majority decision and do their best to make it work. Where they will not, the leader has to balance the disruption of the group against the gains stemming from the majority decision. Such conflicts between the values of unity and harmony on the one hand, and the onward call to advance on the other hand, can cause team leaders many thoughtful hours, and there are no easy answers.

The analysis of any group is not a simple matter. Groups are complex in make up and intricate in procedures. But if you are to function effectively – either as leader or participant – it helps if you recognize and understand the personality characteristics of your group as well as the three areas of overlapping need.

KEY POINTS

Here, by way of summary, are ten commandments for managing communication in groups:

- Keep the objectives of all meetings clearly in mind.
- Plan meetings carefully – decide who is to be present, circulate the agenda and any relevant information in advance.
- Ensure that all, and only, the necessary people are present.
- Agree time limits in advance, and start on time. Try to hold the meetings in a room with a clock.
- Plan the agenda carefully, allocating specific amounts of time to each item. Include time to establish the aims of the meeting, ensure effective discussion, reach conclusions and agree the necessary actions.
- Ensure that, when minutes are necessary, these are concise and definite, and include reference to who is to do what, and by when.
- End meetings on a positive note, summarizing decisions taken and action to be implemented.
- Remember, as chairman, to blend the two roles of referee and leader.
- Analyse your performance as chairman regularly, and be prepared to solicit feedback so that you can develop your skills.
- Review regular meetings from time to time. Make sure that they are necessary, and that the right people are there.

> But of a good leader, who talks little,
> When his work is done, his aim fulfilled,
> They will all say, 'We did this ourselves.'
>
> *Lao Tzu*

ORGANIZATIONS: THE HIMALAYAS OF COMMUNICATION

It was just the day for Organizing Something, or for Writing a
Notice signed Rabbit . . . It was a Captainish sort of day, when
everybody said 'Yes, Rabbit' and 'No, Rabbit' and waited until
he had told them.

A. A. Milne, *The House at Pooh Corner* (1928)

Organizations are the end-results of this Rabbit-like faculty
in human nature of Organizing Something. To organize is
to arrange systematically for a definite purpose. Doubtless
Rabbit had something temporary in mind, like organizing
a picnic. But organizing can and does produce the more
permanent social structures we nowadays call organizations.
A. A. Milne hints at two of their other characteristics
besides permanence: hierarchy and formal communication.
Let us consider each in turn.

Hierarchy
Large human organizations are rarely created at a stroke of
the pen. They tend to evolve organically from working
groups or teams, which in turn come about through the
leadership of one or two people.

A team is an organization in microcosm. It is a whole

made up of interdependent parts, each with its proper function, evolved to achieve a purpose that one person could not attain alone or unaided. The 'parts' in this case are other individuals.

In an organization, the 'parts' are themselves teams or workgroups. Often the transition from working group to larger organization is by a process of rapid or slow organic growth. At some stage or another, Rabbits are employed to give the Something that has evolved some systematic arrangement or organization. The critical factor here is the identification or creation of a hierarchy. 'It was a Captainish sort of day . . .'

Often organizers out to bring order into relative chaos do have some predetermined scheme in mind, such as the military system. But the military system merely reflects a more primitive or natural method of social ordering in large groups, which can be expressed as a simple model:

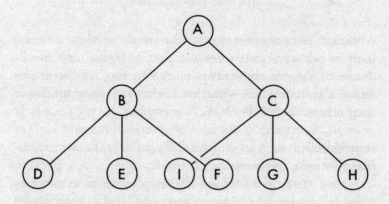

Figure 10.1 *Elementary hierarchy*

Here A has overall leadership responsibility. Three team leaders report directly to B and C, who report in turn directly to A. All the elements of hierarchy are here. We have some rather cumbersome Latin-based words to describe where people come in the structure or order thus created:

Subordinates	B and C are subordinate to A; all the others are subordinate to B and C as well; and the team members in each of the six groups are subordinate to their leaders, and all above.
Coordinates	B and C are coordinate with each other, as are D, E, I, F and G. Team members are also coordinates within teams.
Superordinates	All the named leaders are superordinates, A being obviously the ultimate superordinate

Although *hierarchy* comes from the Greek word for a ruling body of priests organized into orders or ranks, each subordinate to the one above it, it sounds in English like *higher* archy, a system where some are higher and some are lower than others. This UP–DOWN metaphor is very strong. It gives us, for example, the idea of several horizontal *levels* of responsibility, each accompanied (eventually if not immediately) by rank and status.

Notice that hierarchy (or higherarchy) runs counter to tribal life where people are on the same level as their leader and there are no interpositions of other levels. The tribal structure looks more like this:

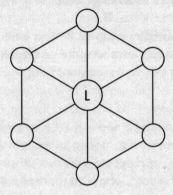

Figure 10.2 *The tribal structure*

In a Bedouin tribe, for example, the sheikh pitches his tent in the middle, and keeps an open door to all-comers. Members of the tribe are essentially free and equal, although in larger tribes there were sub-groups of families or kin. Yet all have the right to take complaints or problems to the paramount sheikh for arbitration or solution.

Originally we were all tribal and the tribal tradition has been deeply influential. For example, it is the matrix of modern democracy. When then has the hierarchical organization prevailed? Sheer size as tribes multiply into nations was one reason. The other reason was military necessity. Armed tribal hordes turned into disciplined armies only as and when they accepted the principle of hierarchy.

ORGANIZING THE PEOPLE

One day, while the tribes of Israel were in the desert, Jethro saw his son-in-law Moses sitting alone with people standing around him from morning till evening, counselling them and solving disputes.

'This is not the best way to do it,' said Jethro. 'You will only wear yourself out and wear out all the people who are here. The task is too heavy for you; you cannot do it by yourself. Now listen to me . . .' Jethro told him that he must remain the people's representative before God and instruct them in the principles of how to behave and what to do. 'But you must yourself search for capable God-fearing men among all the people, honest and incorruptible men, and appoint them over the people as officers over units of a thousand, of a hundred, of fifty or ten. They shall sit as a permanent court for the people; they must refer difficult cases to you but decide simple cases themselves. In this way your burden will be lightened, and they will share it with you. If you do this, God will give you strength, and you will be able to go on. And, moreover, this whole people will here and now regain peace and harmony.'

Two strands have become confused in this story: the establishment of a court of justice and organization for military purposes.

It follows that nations like the Greeks and Romans, who were willing to subject themselves to the discipline of organizations, could conquer tribes or tribal federations in battle. The Roman Army is still the copybook example or model of a very large organization.

Formal communication

Lyndall F. Urwick concluded in *Organization* (1966) that this concept means: 'the arrangements for formal communication in any purposive system of human co-operation in which unity of action cannot be secured by personal contact, custom or social sentiment'.

Now with a small group or team as a leader you can communicate by informal personal contact. But organization implies that you communicate through formal channels, such as a military chain of command. A corollary is that if you work in organizations you have to respect these formal channels.

That doesn't mean to say that *informal* communication is totally absent from organizations – that is far from the case. There is plenty of information discussion, conversation and networking in most organizations. But they should be essentially supplementary. If informal communication dominates it is probably because the formal communication system – the core of the organization – isn't working well.

As we saw in the Case of NETMA Ltd (Chapter 2), *size* and *geographical spread* always put a strain on an organization's power to communicate effectively. If *rapid change* is thrown into the equation the situation can be worse. For conditions of change call for *better* communication, whereas size, geographical spread and much of change itself is working against you.

To overcome the potential problems you need a practical philosophy of communication which embraces the *content* of communication, the *directions* it must take, and your *personal responsibility*.

CONTENT

If you have accepted the three-circles model or general theory of teams and organizations you have a ready-made definition of what people need or want as far as communication is concerned. Let me briefly remind you of the model.

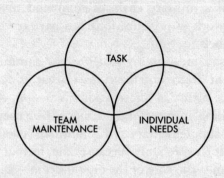

Figure 10.3 *The three circles*

According to the theory, there are *three* areas of need present in working groups and organizations:

- to achieve the common task
- to be held together or to maintain themselves as cohesive unities
- the needs which individuals bring with them into the group

The main *content* of communication – information, ideas and knowledge, etc. – in your organization should tie in with these three overlapping areas. Here I am concentrating on communication Inside the Egg. Of course, members of any organization will be communicating Outside the Egg as well, to customers, clients, suppliers and the public in some shape or form. The internal communication needs are as follows:

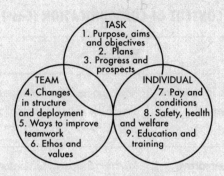

Figure 10.4   *Communication in the three circles*

CONTENT OF COMMUNICATION	
AREA	**NOTES**
1 Purpose, aim and objectives	The core *purpose*, the key *aims* and the more tangible *objectives* are central in communication. Purpose answers *Why*
2 Plans and policies	Planning answers the questions *What, When, How, Where* and *Who*
3 Progress and prospects	Progress motivates – prospects motivate even more, e.g. new products, other innovations and positive changes in the pipeline

CONTENT OF COMMUNICATION (Cont)	
AREA	**NOTES**
4 Changes in structure and deployment	Any organizational changes or alterations in the organization's deployment
5 Ways to improve teamwork	Anything that results in better teamworking, so that the various parts work in an integrated, harmonious whole.
6 Ethos and values	The particular stars the organization steers by in the form of its corporate values; its spirit as opposed to its form
7 Pay and conditions	Anything that affects the remuneration, conditions of work, or personal prospects for employment of individuals
8 Safety, health and welfare	Information that affects safety or security
9 Education and training	Whatever may contribute to the personal development – present competence and future capability – of each individual member.

Figure 10.5

The above list is not exhaustive, but it covers the guts of what people working in organizations both need to know and expect to know. People look out for a vision to inspire their work, a sense of belonging to an interdependent and high-performance team, and for information that improves their sense of value as individuals in this large organization.

SHARE YOUR INFORMATION

Poor leaders hold on to information as a source of power and control. Jan Carlson of Scandinavian Airlines says: 'An individual without information cannot take responsibility. An individual with information cannot help but take responsibility.' Good leaders see the value in sharing information to improve decision making.

DIRECTIONS OR FLOWS

Communication is more than words: it is the imparting of meaning – voluntarily or involuntarily – and it flows.

The most obvious direction of flow is DOWNWARDS from the top to the bottom, or, if you prefer it, from the CENTRE to the PERIPHERY. Imagine a military command post, for example, where the general briefs his commanders, who in turn brief their captains. There are three levels of leadership at work here: *strategic*, *operational* and *team*.

You can see that there is a formal communication structure in place to transmit and translate the general's battle plan into action.

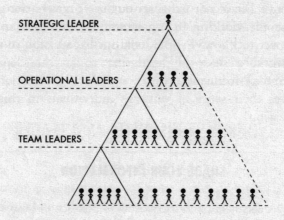

STRATEGIC LEADER

OPERATIONAL LEADERS

TEAM LEADERS

Figure 10.6 *Three levels of leadership*

In the past, however, the above system has not been so good for UPWARD communication. What, you may ask, does a common soldier have to say to a general anyway? The answer was not much. Better armies and navies did introduce constitutional systems for the upward transmission of grievances – never easy because your immediate superior was often the source of your grievance and had no interest in passing your complaints upwards! In Nelson's enlightened navy, for example, every sailor had the right to approach an admiral directly and make a verbal or written complaint or grievance.

What has changed out of all recognition is the nature of operations. Now everyone has the responsibility of passing upwards any relevant information about, for instance, product performance or quality, customer needs or the responses of competitors. Communication has become a two-way traffic.

The same competitive pressures have put a premium on

teamwork. That in turn sorts out the organizations which have gone SIDEWAYS, or lateral communications from those who still have brick walls instead of chalk lines, dividing them like bulkheads into a series of watertight departments or businesses.

YOUR RESPONSIBILITY AS A LEADER

Change throws up the need for leaders; leaders tend to create change. So never complain about change if you are a leader: it is what you are there for! It isn't all about change, however, for you have to balance it against the interests of continuity. So that calls for judgement on the direction, scope and pace of change.

Leadership and communication cannot be separate either. Can you think of a good leader who is not a good communicator? Therefore it is leadership which stitches together the needs for effective change and good communication.

The first step is to see yourself in a role that requires DOWNWARD, UPWARD and SIDEWAYS communication. Even as a strategic leader, you need to be able to communicate upwards to the board of directors or its equivalent. The content of what you communicate should always be relatable to the three circles. Some of it will be self-generated – your vision, your ideas or your plans. But much of your work will be as a channel of communication for information coming from other sources which you have a duty to pass on by virtue of your appointment. How should you do it?

As a general principle, the *high-priority information should go by the best method of communication, which is face to face backed by writing*.

As a leading insurance broker told me: 'It is no accident that for hundreds of years the basic method of transacting business in markets has been face-to-face confrontation between the principals subsequently ratified by written contract, because by this method one can achieve the three criteria of good communication, namely that it should be clear, quick and include a response. It is a personal contact and relationships which count, and the market system would not operate without it.' As trust declines, so does communication at this level.

You should develop an unerring sense both of priorities – Aneurin Bevan once said that '75 per cent of politics is priorities – and the most appropriate methods for their communication.'

Some parameters are needed to enable managers to determine their priorities. May I suggest again the now-familiar concentric circles of priority as an aid, based on the 'need to know' principle.

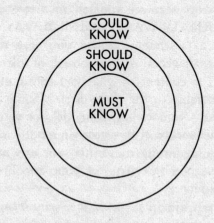

Figure 10.7 *Priorities of 'need to know'*

- MUST KNOW: vital points
- SHOULD KNOW: desirable but not essential
- COULD KNOW: relatively unimportant

MUST KNOW, for example, might include the introduction of a new product (downwards), the probability for good reason, for missing an important and agreed deadline (upwards), or the interest of a major customer in a service offered by a colleague's department (sideways). You might communicate these in a meeting or over the telephone, backed by the necessary paperwork. The fortunes of the organization's football team, as a COULD KNOW, should be left to the noticeboard or newsletter. SHOULD KNOW material should be mainly written or available on the computer screen: you ought to ensure that face-to-face communication − expensive in terms of time and money − is reserved for essential, important or strategic messages and information in each of the three circles and NOT just the task.

I say that because all the pressures are on managers to reduce communication to short-term and bottom-line issues. That is one reason why the world now needs business leaders, not managers.

'Good morning, welcome to this full English breakfast. From the rumours you may have heard you will all know why you are here. For two months a team from our head office in Dayton, Ohio, have been assessing us. You will have seen them in the corridors and accessing your computers. Two breakfasts have been arranged, one tomorrow for those who are staying and this one . . . Please do not return to your offices, the security staff are clearing out your personal possessions. The Managing Director has just telephoned in to say that he has overslept, so I will hand you straight over to our solicitor who will outline the legal minimum of redundancy terms we are forced to give you . . .'

'This should be called the Last Supper,' said Sally grimly to her neighbour as she pushed away her plate. 'Somehow I don't feel like bacon and eggs this morning. Pass the black coffee.'

Many organizations are so tempted – and succumb – to hiring people on short-term contracts and getting rid of them when they cease to need them. Whether or not you can make people redundant and still stay within the framework of the three circles philosophy depends on *why* you do it and *how* you do it.

'You talk about the three circles, John, as a new philosophy of organizations. But how are you meeting the individual needs circle when you make someone redundant? Aren't you being idealistic?' 'Not at all,' I replied. 'Few companies can guarantee people life-long employment. When United Biscuits – a company very committed to good leadership – closed down its Liverpool factory a few years ago, the trade unions complimented them publicly in the press on the way they did it.'

An organization committed to good leadership will manage redundancy with sensitivity, providing the maximum financial package (not the least they can get away with) and as much practical help as possible for finding alternative employment. Good communication and mutual trust are essential.

One of the forgotten arts of communication is public speaking in the sense of strategic or operational leaders standing up alone in front of their people and talking to them about task, team and individual agendas, followed by some two-way discussion. Sending messages by fax isn't quite the same!

ENCOURAGING TWO-WAY COMMUNICATION

At times I received advice from friends, urging me to give up or curtail visits to troops. They correctly stated that, so far as the mass of men was concerned, I could never speak, personally, to more than a tiny percentage. They argued, therefore, that I was merely wearing myself out, without accomplishing anything significant, so far as the whole Army was concerned. With this I did not agree. In the first place I felt that through constant talking to enlisted men I gained accurate impressions of their state of mind. I talked to them about anything and everything: a favourite question of mine was to inquire whether the particular squad or platoon had figured out any new trick or gadget for use in infantry fighting. I would talk about anything so long as I could get the soldier to talk to me in return.

I knew, of course, that news of a visit with even a few men in a division would soon spread throughout the unit. This, I felt, would encourage men to talk to their superiors, and this habit, I believe, promotes efficiency. There is, among the mass of individuals who carry the rifles in war, a great amount of ingenuity and initiative. If men can naturally and without restraint talk to their officers, the products of their resourcefulness becomes available to all. Moreover, out of the habit grows mutual confidence, a feeling of partnership that is the essence of esprit de corps. An army fearful of its officers is never as good as one that trusts and confides in its leaders.

General Dwight D. Eisenhower

It is sometimes difficult to get people together in this way, especially if you are not the chief executive. But you should seize every opportunity of talking – and listening – to any significant groups of those who report indirectly to you.

There are frequent attempts, some more successful than others, to systematic downward, upward and sideways communication by a series of regular meetings, such as briefing groups, liaison committees and works councils. Sometimes legislation directs managers to introduce a particular system, such as works councils.

EUROPEAN WORKS COUNCIL DIRECTIVE

The European Works Council Directive (EWC) will apply, with effect from 22 September 1996, to all companies meeting the criteria within the 14 states (EU 15 minus UK), plus the other EEA states of Norway, Iceland and Liechtenstein. The intention of the Directive is that undertakings with over 1000 employees in the above 17 states, of whom 150 work in each of two or more of these Member States, should establish a European Works Council or procedure to enable them regularly to inform and consult employees via employee representatives.

Despite the fact that the UK has officially opted out, the following UK companies have already announced that they have established Councils: **Marks & Spencer, Pilkington, Courtaulds, United Biscuits, BP Oil and Coats Viyella. GKN, Group 4, ICI, Redland, NatWest Bank, Clarks Shoes** and no doubt others, have negotiations under way. These are all UK companies which, within the criteria of the Directive, are obliged to set up a Works Council for their employees in two or more of the 17 states, and which felt it prudent to include their UK employees in the arrangements.

Many UK employers feel that it makes no sense at all to leave British employees out. In fact more companies are setting up voluntary systems to consult employees before the legislation comes into force. This advice is based on **Article 13(1) of the Directive** which states that the Directive will not apply where 'there is already an agreement, covering the entire workforce, providing for the transnational information and consultation of employees'.

Successful organizations over the years have found it to be good business voluntarily to have sound information and consultation arrangements in place, together with the employee welfare programmes which most of these Directives are emulating.

There is always a temptation to believe that when you have introduced a *system* – such as briefing groups or works councils – you have solved the communication problem. But systems are subject to the law of atrophy: they tend to waste away. Systems can help, but they are as good as the people operating them. The winning combination is simple but durable systems peopled by committed and skilled communicators.

Three possible aims for such consultative or representative meetings are:

- to give employees a chance to improve decisions by contributing comments before decisions are made
- to make the fullest possible use of their experience and ideas in the efficient running of the enterprise
- to give management and employees the opportunity to understand each other's views and objectives

Characteristically these are meetings where discussion takes place on any matter influencing the effectiveness or efficiency of the enterprise prior to decisions being made. Sometimes the group's views will be passed upwards; sometimes the decision will be made by the manager on the spot and in the presence of those who have contributed to his or her judgement.

When managers do not listen they cease to be business leaders and revert to their former status as hired business administrators. So-called managers of this low calibre hardly listen at all: they *ignore*, *forget*, *distort* or *misunderstand* much of what they hear.

A large manufacturing company called Portland Power Units Ltd, makers of diesel engines, decide to invest in a large extension covering the adjacent car park. Mark Evans, the new manager in charge, drew up an elaborate plan for the change so as to minimize any disruption of production as the walls were knocked down. He rearranged the schedules and ordered the new machinery from a firm who had supplied them last time. The result was chaotic. The team leaders on the shop floor said they had not been consulted and the building works would certainly hold up an important new order for China. The union said that the shift schedules were unworkable. 'They could also have saved a lot of money and technical problems if they ordered the new German machinery we saw when we toured that plant in Frankfurt,' added one of the team leaders. Evans finally had to agree that he had not listened to those who knew most about the machinery, the layout of the new extension, the shift schedules or the timetable for building works. His poor listening cost Portland Power Units just under two million pounds. He is now working for another organization – possibly yours.

Consultative meetings may be distinguished from formal management/union discussions on such topics as wage systems, job evaluation, hours of work, holidays and holiday pay. In the last instance elected representatives of work people in trade unions are seeking to reach formal agreement on matters relating to the 'individual needs' circle in the trefoil of three circles model (page 232). In consultations the active working members of an organization are being asked to contribute towards decisions mainly in the field of the common purpose, aims and objectives, and the shape of the structural organization necessary to achieve those short- and long-term ends. As the circles overlap it is not always possible in practice to separate matters of concern for trade unions from those which belong to the individual as a member of a particular organization. But there is a distinction, and it is worth bearing it in mind.

It is usually assumed that a consultative group, formalized into a consultative committee, should exist on a factory or plant basis, although in very large organizations there may be a case for regional, national or international councils. Normally one might find one joint consultation committee, consisting of representatives from management and shop floor, in a factory employing perhaps 1000 men and women or more. Thus it would act as a forum of debate, rather than as a cabinet for decision. Except in schemes for industrial democracy, where the committee becomes the governing council, the final decisions and the ultimate accountability will rest with the board of directors.

Remember that part of your skill as a communicator is to be aware of feedback – the part of your input that bounces back to you. It is useful because it helps you to judge whether or not communication is likely to be effective. Initial feedback – positive or negative – must be distinguished from the effect of the message as a whole (see page 29). 'It is interesting,' one chief executive told me, 'that in business dealings we expect, and generally get, a response to every communication even though it be only an acknowledgement for a cheque; but in staff matters we are very often content to put a notice on the board and leave it at that.'

One of the advantages of getting out of your office (if you still have one) and going around talking to people is that you can gauge the flow of communication as it courses through the arteries and veins of the network:

- Did that message you asked operational leaders to brief to their team leaders reach *this* team in another country?
- Why didn't this key suggestion for a new extension of service to existing major customers get communicated to the senior leadership team?
- How come that our Holland branch have cracked this particular production problem six months ago, but when I was in Spain last week they were still struggling with it?
- Why hasn't this young graduate manager in Scotland heard about our new leadership development strategy?
- Don't these rumours and false reports suggest that we are falling down in communication? Is it a systems problem or a people problem?

Like the systems mentioned above, information technology – computers, fax, E-mail, television link-ups, mobile radios and video – will not solve your communication problems, they are only aids. Only by developing leaders at all three levels, and persuading them to work together as a team, will your organization be able to face the challenges of change and growth with confidence.

KEY POINTS

- To organize implies arranging so that the whole aggregate works as a unit with each element having a proper function. In social bodies hierarchy and formal communication play a key role. Organizations are formal communication systems, open to their environment, with a definite purpose.

- The necessary content of communication within an organization is suggested by the three circles:
  TASK: the common purpose or vision, aims and objectives, strategy and plans, future prospects.
  TEAM: issues to do with changes in organization or team work, how we can work better together.
  INDIVIDUAL: anything that affects the individual for better or worse.

- Staying within the familiar spatial metaphor, there are three main directions of flows of communication: DOWNWARD, UPWARD and SIDEWAYS. In times past, the emphasis fell on downwards communication from high to low. Now, for a variety of reasons, the formal communication system – supplemented by the informal one – has to bear information and ideas in *all three directions*. Therefore it has to become much more flexible in the future.

- As a general principle, high-priority information (the MUST as opposed to SHOULD or COULD know) should go by the best method of communication, which is face to face backed by the written word.

- As a leader you should not only place a high premium on good communication but become skilled in using the right method for it. Your role or appointment contains an inbuilt requirement to communicate in all three directions. In each direction you may be communicating self-generated ideas or acting as a transmitter – the latter is as important as the former.

● Systems, such as briefing groups or joint consultative councils, can all contribute, but remember that it is easier to set them up than to maintain them at a high level of effectiveness? Nor will information technology solve all your communication problems. Good communication requires good communicators. Which brings it back to YOU!

The major mistake in communication is to believe that it happens.
George Bernard Shaw

INDEX

Visit **www.panmacmillan.com** to read more about all our books and to buy them. You will also find features, author interviews and news of any author events, and you can sign up for e-newsletters so that you're always first to hear about our new releases.

www.panmacmillan.com

GIFT SELECTOR
YOUR ACCOUNT
WISH LIST
WAITING LIST

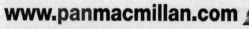

HOME | ABOUT US | IMPRINTS | TRADE/MEDIA | CONTACT US | ADVANCED SEARCH | SEARCH [ ] GO

BOOK CATEGORIES | WHAT'S NEW | AUTHORS/ILLUSTRATORS | BESTSELLERS | READING GROUPS

Coming Soon...

Reading Groups

Competitions
Feeling Lucky?

Extracts
Sneak Previews

Interviews

Events
Meet Our Stars

Reviews
What The Critics Say

News & Awards

Editor's Choice
What We're Reading